# Praise for Loving Allie, Transforming the Journey of Loss

"Dayle Spencer's deeply personal "Loving Allie" offers an insightful and candid look at the cycles of life and death we must all encounter. Whether currently in grief or not, we highly recommend it for all families."

**-Jimmy and Rosalynn Carter**
39th President and Former First Lady
United States of America
NY Times Best Selling Authors

"Straight from the heart and from the soul of a mother grappling with the unthinkable -- Dayle Spencer tells her story "Loving Allie" with generosity and courage, leaving the reader the transcendent power of love. Interspersed with stories of births which had become haunting takes us on a mother's journey from her daughter's illness and sudden death through the process of healing herself, first to the horror of the initial experience, then, to the people around her. It leaves us certain that this loss and any such loss is yet another story of birth. But whose birth - Allie's; Dayle's; all the dear friends'; ours; or that of all humanity, the entire world and the universe itself?

In showing us the road taken past her heartbreaking experience, Ms. Spencer provides a transformative view of the full cycle of life we are all a part of and shows us how we might appreciate and love it, even when it comes at us in ways that are different from what we want or expect."

**-Beth M. Karassik, Ph.D.**
Clinical Psychologist
Founder, The Close

"Dayle Spencer delivers a powerful love letter, a gut wrenching outpouring of grief, and a possible guide to all of us dealing with the loss of someone we'd never thought we could lose. She stands naked in front of strangers, her husband, her daughter, her mother and then finally herself & God, to ask a simple and unrelenting question, why? Most books like this never get past the loss, let alone give us front row seats to the operation Dayle does on herself. You may not use this book now, or in the near future but you'll eventually be glad that you read it. It's not just a "mothers journey;" it's everyone's journey.

Thank you Dayle."
**-Louie Anderson**
New York Times Best Selling Author
Comedian

"In Dayle Spencer's poignant story of losing her only daughter we are invited to share her painful journey from sudden inexplicable tragedy to some fragile sense of acceptance and closure. There had been no protracted illness, no warning signs, no opportunity to be at the bedside for tender words of how much she was loved. After all, who expects a healthy vibrant twenty-eight-year old to die in one of the best hospitals of the flu? The reader follows Ms. Spencer's life from the shattering phone call in the middle of the night through months of blinding grief, disbelief, rage, and the endless details and legalities, to a gradual return to a purposeful life where living and loving are possible again. In her chapter on Lessons Learned the Hard Way, the author gives a valuable primer for any one of us dealing with a crisis or personal tragedy. As a therapist, I highly recommend it. *"Loving Allie"* is an ancient human story of loss; one we all in some way have shared and can learn from."
**-Barbara Findeisen, Psychotherapist**
Past President Association of Prenatal and
Perinatal Psychology and Health
Founder, STAR Foundation

# loving Allie

## Transforming the Journey of Loss

# Dayle E. Spencer

BALBOA.
PRESS

A DIVISION OF HAY HOUSE

Balboa Press books may be ordered through booksellers or by contacting:

Balboa Press
A Division of Hay House
1663 Liberty Drive
Bloomington, IN 47403
www.balboapress.com
1 (877) 407-4847

Printed in the United States of America.

ISBN: 978-1-4525-2194-7 (sc)
ISBN: 978-1-4525-2196-1 (hc)
ISBN: 978-1-4525-2195-4 (e)

Library of Congress Control Number: 2014916171

Balboa Press rev. date: 09/24/2014

ALLISON LANIER POWELL, age 28, beloved daughter of Dayle and William Spencer and Donald W. and Bonny Powell, died Sunday, January 2, 2011, in Boston. Allison was an accomplished theater producer, director, playwright, and performer. For more than twenty-two years she had been in stage performances. Her most recent play was "Choose Thine Own Adventure," which she co-wrote with William Shakespeare. It ran for six weeks of sold-out performances in Chicago in September and October of 2010.

She attended elementary school in Lilburn, Georgia, and then moved to Maui, Hawaii, where she graduated with honors from Seabury Hall. She served as the student body president and performed in many plays while a student there. She graduated *cum laude* from Colgate University in New York, majoring in religion and philosophy. She also studied at St.

Andrews University, Scotland, and in Melbourne, Australia. During her college years she was active in experimental theater and after graduation worked in the San Francisco and Chicago theater communities.

She is also survived by her brother, Geoffrey Taft Powell of Nashville, Tennessee, and stepbrothers Matthew Spencer-Grice of Portland, Oregon, and Daniel, Matthew, and David Phillips of Marietta, Georgia.

A celebration of her life on the stage premiered on Friday, January 14, 2011 at 2 p.m., at the Strand Theater in Marietta, Georgia, with a reception following. It was also simultaneously webcast.

# Acknowledgments

W HERE DO I even begin to say thank you to so many souls who helped me survive this journey? There were such incredible acts of kindness and generosity from many, many people, in numerous countries.

All the people who braved the ice storm of the century to come to Marietta, Georgia, to celebrate Allie's life will forever be in my heart. Those who mounted the stage. Those who sat in the audience. Those who donned the costumes. Those who catered the reception. Those who rehearsed. Those who performed. Those who directed. Those who produced and broadcast the celebration. The folks who were with us, although far removed, but were watching the simultaneous webcast in Hawaii, Australia, New Zealand, Singapore, Egypt, Norway, Germany, and the US mainland are in my heart space as well.

Those who donated to her memorial plaque at Seabury Hall and those who continue to contribute to the Allie Fund at Filament Theatre were generous beyond belief. Those who sent such dear sweet messages, and cards to us even though they couldn't be with us for the celebration. Those who gathered on Maui to hold us and help us when we returned. Those who contributed to the video montage.

Those who loved Allie. Those whom she loved. You know who you are. Allie told you she loved you and you showed her such beautiful love in so many ways.

Those who encouraged me to write my way out of this descent. Those who patiently read my writing and made suggestions on ways to improve it. Those who gave me advance reviews. Those who edited it. Those who helped me publish it.

And to the one, who was with me every step of the way. Who loved me when I couldn't love myself. Who held me when I needed to cry. Who gave me the courage and the support I needed to just keep taking the next step and the next step until we got through it all. To my soul mate, Will. I am so lucky to be loving you.

And to Geoff and Matt, who suffered as well. Whose own stories are worth telling. Maybe someday they will.

And to Winston, who greets each day with such excitement and wonder and showers us with unconditional puppy love.

I am deeply, profoundly grateful.

# Contents

# Allie in a Nutshell

I HAVE STRUGGLED to introduce Allie to the reader in any way that does justice to her wonderful spirit, humor, and joie de vivre. Perhaps her own words, with her unique spellings, in the following email exchange with her friend and former roommate, Liz Ambrosia, capture her better than I ever could.

**A Powell <allison.powell@gmail.com>   Wed, Dec 1, 2010 at 6:31 PM**

To: Son <liz.ambrosia>

I almost had a break down today when I found out subtle, which CLEARLY sounds like "suddle" or even "sutle" or even "sudel" but in no way, shape or form sounds like suBtle---has a B in it for fucks sake. In protest, I refuse to ever say this word again.

**Liz Ambrosia <liz.ambrosia>**        **Wed, Dec 1, 2010 at 11:48 PM**

To: A Powell <allison.powell@gmail.com>

Wait, you've been spelling it like those other ways all this time? How were you finally exposed to the truth? The silent "b" truth sometimes hurts the most...but it will also bring you the most joy, set you free and unleash your inner child.

---

**A Powell <allison.powell@gmail.com>**    **Thu, Dec 2, 2010 at 4:45 AM**

To: Liz Ambrosia <liz.ambrosia>

I don't think I've ever typed the word before or else would have realized what a shit show it is. I almost included it in an essay I'm writing but now, no way. I'm actullay thinking I should start pronouncing it sub-tle in conversations just to see if anyone notices or corrects me--at which point I can correct THEM for going along with the concept of a silent B.

At least with lamb it's at the end of the word---I can understand those getting truncated. But right in the middle?

I just looked it up. Other offenders include: debt, doubt, plumber, (that's a good one. there's a lot of silent B following m. something to think about).

Myabe I'll go as silent B for halloween next year.

# Birth Stories

---

BIRTH STORIES ARE important.

They imprint us for life in small and large ways. It makes a difference to know if we were wanted, planned, a surprise, early, late, easy, complicated, vaginal, caesarian, a multiple, breach, subjected to any traumas while in the womb, or anything else that makes up the story of the beginning of our existence on this earth. If we don't already know the story of our births, we should make it our business to find out what happened to us from the beginning.

Birth stories make for interesting telling, even if they're sad, but especially if they're happy. My own birth story was simple. I was the eighth of ten children, born to a poor family in Anniston, Alabama. My conception was not planned. My parents had nine months to pick out a name for me but didn't. My birth was easy, in a hospital. The nurse named me. I was breast fed like the rest of my siblings. Each of the ten of us was born at intervals of three years, two years, three years, two

3

years, so that every other one of us is five years older. It makes keeping up with our siblings' ages easier.

Because I was born in the middle of the pack, I learned early on how to please others. I learned how to negotiate for what I wanted. Everything was subject to negotiation. If I didn't want to sleep in the middle of three people in a bed, I had to figure out what to trade my two older sisters for one of their outside spots.

I also learned that in order to get any attention I had to be quick, smart, vocal, and competitive. It was easy to be missed in such a large crowd. I learned how to be seen and heard.

Each year on my children's birthdays I call them, usually before they wake up, sing "Happy Birthday" to them, and retell them the story of their births. I tell it so they'll know how much they were wanted, how long we waited for their arrivals, how much they're loved, and how blessed we were by their very existence. In retelling these birth stories I try to recall minute details about how it felt, what time of day it was, and so forth, --small things, that mark their entry into this world as unique.

*Loving Allie* is mostly a death story about the death of my only daughter -- far too soon -- at age twenty-eight, from the flu. Not an exotic strain of the flu. Nothing rare or unusual. Just the simple flu, a virus that kills about thirty-six thousand people annually in the United States.

But more than a death story, it's a life story, about her life and mine. The story of her life begins with her birth story, a story that she heard from me many times, so often, that it became a kind of joke among her roommates and friends, who would sometimes overhear her end of the conversations on those birthdays when she was away from home. I think she loved hearing her birth story each year. In fact, she loved it so much, she began making up birth stories for her friends as well.

When she died, many of those friends participated in a celebration of her life by singing, dancing, telling stories, and more to help us remember Allie and honor her life's journey.

In order to show them how very much their being in her life meant to me, I wrote a kind of mythical birth story for many of them in the months following her death. My husband, Will and I would call each of them and sing to them and then they would receive an email message with their own mythical birth story. Sometimes their mythical birth stories seemed to flow through me, rather than come from me. I like to think I had help from Allie in writing them. When I finished one that seemed rather clever, I smiled and thanked her for sharing it with me so I could pass it on to the ones she loved.

Allie's birth story is told throughout this book. Her friends' birth stories are also included to weave together their lives with hers. Those whose stories are included here were the ones she held dear to her heart, her closest circle from high school, college, and beyond. She chose her friends wisely and kept them close. We couldn't have survived her death without the loving support of so many of her friends. These little birth stories were one way to show them how much they mean to us.

Allie was loved from the moment she was conceived. It was my very great honor to have been given twenty-eight years, eight months, and one week with her in my life.

This is her story, theirs, and mine.

# She Was Not Mine

OH, I GAVE birth to her, make no mistake about that. But that just gave me claim to a special relationship with Allie. We knew each other from start to finish. And even at the start she came into the world in her own signature way, in her own good time.

She was a second child; Geoff was three when she was born. She was planned. She was very much wanted. She was two weeks late and in those last weeks a colleague in the US Attorney's office, where I was working at the time, actually said I looked like a beached whale. I had gained about forty pounds during her pregnancy, seven of those in just one week. And once again, as with Geoff, I worked until her due date before scaling back my hours. In fact, when she was due, I was co-counsel in a rather heated trial involving civil rights violations by police officers. There was a hung jury and a mistrial was granted. One of the jurors, explaining why he held out for an acquittal, said that a pregnant woman had no place in the courtroom.

The judge scheduled the retrial to start when Allie would be just two weeks old. So on the day she was born, FBI agents came to the hospital and sat on the edge of my bed as we reviewed the transcripts from the first trial in preparation for the retrial. She lay sleeping in a bassinet nearby.

Labor lasted thirteen hours and there were no complications. She was a beautiful baby, alert and able to nurse almost instantly upon birth.

During my pregnancy with Allie, her paternal grandmother, Lucille Lanier Powell -- known to all as "Red", due to her fiery hair color -- died. I loved Red and knew that she would have adored having a granddaughter, especially one named for her, so Don and I decided that the new baby would have the middle name Lanier. If it were a girl, it would be Allison Lanier Powell. A boy would have been Douglas Lanier Powell.

Everyone thought it would be another boy. My mother, who herself had ten children and was pretty accurate about such predictions, was betting on a boy based on how I was carrying her. My obstetrician, who had delivered babies for decades, said it was a boy, based on the heartbeat and placement. The technician who gave me the sonogram thought she saw a penis and called it a boy. And all the delivery room personnel, experts all, were convinced it would be a boy when they connected the fetal monitor during delivery.

In my heart of hearts, I wanted a daughter. I had a son. I loved him deeply. He was healthy, happy, and a joy to us all. But I wanted a girl. I wanted a child like me, one whose moods I would understand, one whom I could parent through the maze of girlhood and womanhood. I know now that this was merely egotism on my part. It reflected a narcissistic desire to perpetuate my own image in the world. I was looking for a mini-me. I had vain images of mother-daughter look-alike outfits. I had notions that I would pick her clothes, style her hair, and teach her all the things I wanted her to learn.

I had so underestimated the life force that would come into this world on April 26, 1982, weighing eight pounds and thirteen ounces, who would be named Allison Lanier Powell. She was a Taurus. A bull. Strong-willed. From the age of two she refused to allow me to dress her or even pick out her clothes. She would leave the house each day reflecting her style and her tastes, not mine.

In the movie *Out of Africa*, when Robert Redford's character, Denys Finch Hatton, dies, Meryl Streep's character, Karen Blixen, gives the graveside eulogy. She said, "Now take back the soul of Denys George Finch Hatton, whom You have shared with us. He brought us joy ... and we loved him well. He was not ours. He was not mine."

Allie taught me that lesson over and over again. She had no interest in studying law, thanks very much. For her the stage and performing arts held more interest than courtroom dramas. She often told me that she had no intention of ever giving me grandchildren. In fact, she had serious issues with the idea of even getting married. No man would ever give her away at the altar. She was not chattel to be given. If she should deign to marry, it would be on her terms, not based on any traditional approach to weddings or married life.

Although these rebuffs were painful to me, they were also a source of maternal pride. I, too, had been forced to be strong to survive my own childhood poverty. From the age of fifteen I was never not employed. From eighteen on, I was self-sufficient, working my way through both college and law school. Although the eighth child in my family, I was the first to go to college and the only one to obtain a graduate degree. Just after college, I sued my employer for sex discrimination in the workplace and won. That money paid for my first year's tuition in law school. I was the first pregnant federal prosecutor in the history of the State of Alabama. A criminal I prosecuted once dubbed me the Big Blonde Bitch, and the label stuck. So I knew something of a woman's need to be strong-willed.

I knew that Allie would have to be strong and independent to make it in the world; I just didn't understand that sometimes that would also have to include rejecting me. She chose to attend college in New York, about as far away from our home in Maui as she could go. As a young adult, she chose to live in places like San Francisco, Melbourne, Chicago, and Boston, all at least a few thousand miles from home. She decided to stop coming home for Thanksgiving because it was important that she and her friends all be together for the holiday, creating their own traditions.

Some of her individuality may be traced to her rites of passage ceremony that my Star Sisters and I created for her on her twelfth birthday. In my mind, this marked the moment when Allie no longer doubted who she was in the world and what she was capable of manifesting.

Girls get their first menses, or menarche, under many different circumstances. I remember being afraid when I found blood in my panties for the first time, although my sister, Carolyn, who was two years older, had told me it would happen. It was scary and weird. My family's approach was to say nothing. Just before my oldest sister, Patricia, got married at age eighteen, she asked our mother to tell her what she needed to know about being a wife. My mom replied that anything she needed to know she could read about in the Bible. It was taboo to talk about sex in our family, although, judging from the numbers, a lot of it must have been going on. So when I started my first period, alone and afraid, Carolyn just gave me an inch-thick sanitary napkin and showed me how to hook it into an elastic belt-like structure (which they no longer even make) and it was up to me to sort out my own feelings about the whole womanhood matter.

Years later, when I started dating Don Powell as a junior in college, I was invited to spend the weekend at his family home in Birmingham, sixty miles away. Even though I was over eighteen, living on campus, and paying for all my college expenses, I still felt obligated to secure my parents' permission for such a bold step. All our lives we had never been allowed to sleep over at any of our friends' homes. It was another family taboo, an inflexible rule. So, dutiful daughter that I was, I felt that I needed their okay to go. I went home for the weekend for the express purpose of asking their permission for this bold step.

Neither of my parents had graduated from high school. (Well, actually my mother did graduate at age seventy-two, but that's another story.) They got married when my mother was fifteen and my dad was seventeen. My dad worked a number of jobs, including driving a school bus and a taxi, working in a foundry, and selling fresh fruits and vegetables. He often had a day job and a night job, and he wanted to come home to a hot meal at the end of the shift. My mother was a stay at home mom who sold everything from punches on bingo cards to catalog order shoes and blankets. And she cooked three meals a day with homemade biscuits at every one of them. She used the same wooden bread bowl and same bread pan to make those biscuits every single day.

So, on Saturday morning, after breakfast when my Dad had just finished his night shift and was ready to go to bed, I sprang the question on them. Could I go home with Don the next weekend and spend the weekend with his family? I tried to ask it as innocently as I possibly could.

Of course the immediate answer was *NO*.

*Why not?* I asked. His parents would be there. We wouldn't be alone. They were very nice people.

Again, *NO.*

*I don't understand why this is such a big deal,* I replied. *It is no different than being on campus together.*

My dad had had enough. He stood up. Picked up the greasy biscuit pan and began rubbing his hand on the outside of the pan while yelling at me.

*"Don't you know you can only rub two bricks together for just so long before you get a spark?"*

Now, I knew exactly what he meant by that but I wasn't going to let him know I knew because the whole point of this discussion was to convince them that nothing inappropriate was going to happen if I did go to Birmingham.

So, I tried my best to look confused and puzzled, and then replied, *"I have no idea what you are talking about."*

And, as far as I can remember that was the first time the taboo was broken in our family. My father threw down that biscuit pan and bellowed at me,

*"I ---*
*MEAN ---*
*SEX, ---*
*DAMN IT!!!!!!!"*

Well, I did go to Birmingham that weekend. Nothing untoward happened. And a year later I married Don.

I wanted my children to grow up in an environment that was better than mine had been and I wanted them, especially my daughter, to know her true worth as a woman and so I looked to my Star Sisters to help me give her that grounding as she was about to become a woman.

My Star Sisters, Lea Flocchini, Nancy Miner, and Christa Huseby, had become dear friends of mine when we went through a transformative personal development program together in 1993. We have been joined at the hip and the heart ever since and each year, for the past twenty years, we have met for a reunion. Between us we have been through so many monumental life changes together and we have always been there for each other to listen, to hold, to support. So naturally, it was to my Star Sisters that I turned when I needed to create a rite of passage for Allison's entry into womanhood.

Lea, who is from Idaho, has done a lot of counseling work herself and is wonderful at creating sacred ceremonies, including marriages. Christa, who splits her time between Nashville and Florida, has the perspective of being older than me with grown children and grandchildren. She had been there, done that. Nancy, who lives in Arkansas, is an artist and animal activist and playful and child-like in her innocence. Allie knew all of my Star Sisters and loved them as well, especially Nancy, whom she adored.

I had told Allie that we were going to do something very special for her twelfth birthday. She knew that it involved a road trip with the Star Sisters. She thought that was pretty weird to be going away with a bunch of middle-aged women, but she was game to try it.

The plan was to take her away to a remote cabin in the north Georgia mountains and induct her into womanhood in a ceremonial way that empowered her, rather than allow her to just stumble through as I did, or be frightened by the changes in her body or her emotions as she developed. The Star Sisters all flew to Atlanta, where we were living at the time. I met them at the airport and we stopped to pick up a dozen red roses for

Allie before heading to her middle school to kidnap her for the weekend.

I had studied rites of passage ceremonies used by indigenous societies. I knew that many social systems had developed rituals to mark the important transitions in life. They might involve vision quests, scarification, isolation, celebrations, etc. My own tribe, my family, had none. We were part Cherokee, but somehow along the way, we had lost that meaning and identity that comes from marking important passages ritually. Having been through such ceremonies in parts of Africa, and having attended bar and bat mitzvahs I really wanted us to design some meaningful passage for Allie.

So we Star Sisters went to Shiloh Middle School on her twelfth birthday, April 26, 1994, and withdrew her from class. We gave her the red roses and told her that we were going to take her away and tell her all about being a woman. We would answer any of her questions honestly and candidly. No subject would be taboo for her. We wanted to prepare her for menses without fear, sex without guilt, and womanhood with a sense of her own power.

I did not know it at the time I rented the cabin, but I later learned that the place we were taking her was in fact Blood Mountain, a sacred site to the Cherokee people. It is the tallest elevation on the Georgia section of the Appalachian Trail. All I knew was that we could rent a quiet cabin in the woods and there were waterfalls and hiking trails we could use.

In that cabin we each presented Allie with a small bead that symbolized this passage in her life. We wove those beads into a necklace to remind her of the experience. We each told her our own stories of entering womanhood. We talked about menses, sex, orgasms, childbirth, breasts, labias, vaginas, cervixes, episiotomies, breast milk, clitorises, acne, and more. We Star

Sisters went for bare breasted hikes up the mountain trail. Allie was totally embarrassed by our brazenness. But the sun felt wonderful. And, at her insistence, we did cover up when other hikers were approaching.

And Lea created a ceremony whereby Allie and I were tied together with twine to represent the umbilical cord that first joined us, and we were each given a pair of scissors. We both spoke to each other with words of love and gratitude for what the other meant in our lives. I told her what an honor it had been to give birth to her and how grateful I was that my prayer to have a daughter was granted. She thanked the Star Sisters and me for this ceremony and said that although it was crazy scary, it was also wonderful.

Each of us, mother and daughter, had to make her own decision to cut the cord. I was releasing her as my little girl, and accepting her into womanhood as my friend and equal. She was letting go of me as her mother and accepting me as her friend and equal. We cut those cords in tears of joy and love.

And, fittingly, Allie got her first menses on the top of Blood Mountain, encircled by four women who loved her. That was an amazing, mind-blowing moment. It was lovely. It was deeply moving. We cried and we laughed and laughed because we knew we would be telling that story for the rest of our lives.

Allie walked up Blood Mountain as a young girl, but she strode down it a strong, empowered young woman, her *own* woman.

# The Birth Story of Patty Tredway

A MYTHICAL BIRTH STORY written for Patty, who was Allie's friend from Colgate and with whom she lived, together with Liz Ambrosia, and Luisa Engel as a self-made family, in San Francisco following their graduation. Patty was the "baby girl" in their family.

Written November 12, 2011

*Pat a cake; pat a cake, baker man.*
*Bake me a cake as fast as you can.*
*Pat it and prick it and mark it with a T,*
*And put it in the oven for baby and me!*

*Dear Patty, or Pattycake, as you are sometimes called,*

*Did you know that for the nine months before your birth, your mother, she of face so fair and heart brimming with love, would sit by the hearth and work a wad of Play Doh into the shape of a pancake while saying this little rhyme over and over again? It became quite the obsession with her as she whiled away the long weeks and months before your birth.*

*Sometimes, the Play Doh cake would be pink, sometimes green, but before tucking it back into its little cardboard container she would hold it to her nose and inhale deeply to savor the sweet smell of Play Doh by the fireside.*

*Now this ritual was actually quite common in the 1980s with pregnant women. Literally millions of women all over the world were also patting Play Doh into little hearthside pancakes. But unlike the rest of those pregnant women, your mother had a secret little ritual she added to the routine. Just before returning her Play Doh to the round tube, she would pinch off a small bite and pop it into her mouth and swallow it!*

*And, as she swallowed and tasted the sweet pinkness or greenness she made wishes.*

*"I wish that my child might be born healthy," she said, and then gulped, one day.*

*"I wish that my child might be kind," then burped, another day.*

*"I wish that my child might be caring and loving," she hoped on yet a different day.*

*And on and on it went. Two hundred eighty days of Play Doh patty cakes, sweet smells, and the taste of pinkness and greenness as she wished with all her heart for your birth.*

*Then, on November 12, 1981, all her wishes were granted, as you made your entry into this world. They swaddled you into a receiving blanket, handed you to your mother, who immediately called you her Patty Cake, and they left your family to bond with its new little baby.*

*And, wouldn't you know it? As your Mom and Dad were drinking in their first looks at their perfect child and they kissed you all over your face, nose, eyes and little tiny fingers, your parents were the first to notice it...*

*A sweet smell of pinkness and greenness wafted over them.*

*Our wonderful Patty, marked with a T, had found her way home.*

*And we have been inhaling your sweetness ever since.*

*Happy 30th Birthday, dear Patty.*

# Hearing the Impossible

2010 HAD BEEN another fast-paced year for my husband Will and me. We were living in Estes Park, Colorado, a small mountain town with more elk than people, and at almost 8,000 feet elevation, with winters that can last for six months. We felt that we needed a change of pace and a new altitude to greet the New Year.

So we planned to drive more than fifteen hundred miles to the Alabama seashore and rent an idyllic house at the beach in January and February of 2011 to give ourselves a much-needed rest and also some peace and quiet to pursue writing projects we had been postponing for too long. What could be more soothing than an empty beach in winter, we thought.

The day after Christmas we stuffed our Toyota Land Cruiser with everything we thought we couldn't live without for two months, including a new kayak and our loyal and constant companion, Guinness, a tri-color Cavalier King Charles. Computers, printers, boxes of research and reference books, cameras, casual beach-walking clothes, and sun hats were all loaded into our car, together with a dog bed, dog cage, and lots of dog toys and treats. We had taken so much stuff that we needed a carrier on top of the car for extra storage and the kayak was strapped to the rooftop as well. Our bicycles were mounted on the rear. Anyone who saw us driving knew we were going to be gone for quite a while.

We stopped in Birmingham, en route to the beach, where I did a half-day workshop for a law firm headed by a classmate of mine, Charlie Waldrep. Birmingham was the town where I attended law school and had later served as a federal prosecutor. It had always been good to me. The workshop took place on December 30th and when it was over we pointed the car due south for Ft. Morgan, Alabama, and our much-needed break. Our journey was nearly at an end. We spent one night en route and arrived at the beach on New Year's Eve.

The house we rented was mammoth, with six bedrooms and even two dishwashers. We had planned to invite a series of friends and family to come visit us there during the weekends. We even planned a mini law school class reunion to celebrate our friendships of more than thirty-five years with seven of my classmates and their spouses. It was a three-story house, built on stilts, and to get to the top floor master bedroom required walking up four flights of stairs. Up and down we went, moving all our cargo from the car to the house. And as soon as all the cargo was unloaded we knew we had to get back in the car to find food and supplies before all the stores closed.

That meant a trip to Bruno's in Gulf Shores for some southern grocery shopping. In Alabama tea is presumed to be sweetened unless written notice is given to the contrary. And Bruno's carried sweet tea by the gallon. They also carried boiled peanuts soaked in brine, Golden Flake potato chips, and

Krispy Kreme Donuts. And did I mention fried chicken? I was like a hog in sunshine, racing through aisle after aisle, loading up on memories of my barefoot childhood. We bought enough food for a small army, and beer, wine, and mixed drinks to last the entire two months. We were done. Finally done.

We slowly drove the twenty-two miles back to the beach house as the sun was setting on the day and the year. As we unloaded the groceries and carried them into the house the winds were howling and sand was blasting our faces and hands but we didn't care. We were finally away from it all and settling in for the longest vacation we had ever taken. 2010 had been a good year and we were happily looking forward to 2011.

Our sons, Matt and Geoff called us during the day to wish us a happy New Year. It was a typical check in with the folks before you go out to celebrate kind of call. They were making sure we had made it safely and everything was okay. We hadn't heard from Allie yet, but it was early still, and she always called. As the day wore on I began to be a little concerned and was actually walking to the phone to call her when it rang.

I have wondered so many times, *what if I hadn't answered the call?* Would the rest have happened as it did? Would it have happened at all? Until I picked up that phone on New Year's Eve, I would have said we led a charmed life. Life was good. We were blessed. We were the lucky ones.

Although it is possible to assign a unique ring tone to signal when a certain person is calling, I didn't need one to know which of my children was on the line. They had predictable patterns for their calls home. And I knew before answering that this call was from Allie. I even answered the phone, "Baby Girl!" knowing that the next voice I heard would belong to my beautiful, twenty-eight year-old daughter, Allison Lanier Powell.

Except that it didn't. It was actually John Meagher calling. John was Allie's more than boyfriend, less than fiancé. They had dated off and on for several years and only the week before, at Christmas, Allie had moved from Chicago to Boston to live with John. She was quite conflicted about the move. She didn't want to compromise on her principles, including independence. She had been self-sufficient since graduating from college four years earlier and this decision to live with John included her absolute insistence that she would get a job and contribute fully to their expenses. Allie was adept at getting jobs since winning the job interview competition in her Middle School. She was bright, articulate, and, due to her theatrical experiences, could spontaneously create an image of her ability that was persuasive to almost every potential employer she met. But since she had only been in Boston one week, and that was the week of Christmas, her job search was postponed until the start of the New Year.

The grand scheme was that the move to Boston was only temporary anyway. She had applied to graduate school in several cities and the deal she and John struck was that when (not if) she was accepted they would both move to whatever location was necessary for her to pursue a Master's Degree in Theatre and Performing Arts. John's willingness to be part of her career path was one of the many things that endeared him to her. Another was his high tolerance for costumes and all things glittery.

I had first met John in San Francisco, where he had lived two blocks away from Allie and her posse. John and Allie met at a neighborhood block party and although there was a definite attraction, it was not love at first sight. They had bantered throughout the party and at the end of the evening he finally worked up the nerve to ask her for her phone number, assuming that it was a foregone conclusion. But her deep blue eyes got round and wide and she told him that she had seen him kissing another girl at the party just a couple of hours before, so no, she would not give him her phone number. She did one of her famous pivots and exited, stage left. John is persistent, however, and he eventually tracked her down and won her heart.

I knew they were serious when I visited Allie in San Francisco some time later. She was working as the business manager at a theater on the wharf at Pier 39 where *Menopause the Musical* was playing. My plan was to see my daughter and her play on the same trip.

Allie lived with three of her best friends, all of whom had attended Colgate University together, Patty Tredway, Liz Ambrosia, and Luisa Engel. The girls, as I came to think of them, had bravely decided after graduation that they wanted to live together and that San Francisco would be an ideal place to be single young adults. Although none of them had a job prospect, or any family living there, they just piled their possessions into one car (donated by Patty's father) and made the cross-country trip together. When they arrived they went straight to an apartment that they had found on craigslist. As luck would have it, it was located above a restaurant. And so they popped into the small restaurant and introduced themselves to the wait staff and bartenders. Before the night was over, the restaurant staff had fed them a free meal, helped unload the car, moved them into their small first apartment and even given jobs to two of the girls. They did not lack for chutzpah!

Over the years that the girls lived in San Francisco, the rule was that any time their parents came to town the parents took the whole house out to dinner together. Will and I enjoyed these family dinners with the girls on each visit. But when I first met

John, I had come by myself. It was near the date of my birthday in late May and John, who had clearly been briefed on what to expect, seemed rather nervous.

Keeping with the house tradition, I took Allie, John, Liz, and Patty to dinner together before seeing *Menopause the Musical*. John gave me flowers for my birthday, an endearing touch. Then we proceeded to Fisherman's Wharf for the sold-out performance. Allie had to be backstage, but she had managed to save seats for us in the middle of the third row. And she had also planned for John to be singled out by the cast and made a part of the performance. The cast thoroughly embarrassed John, one of the few men in the audience, and he rolled with each punch line. I came to appreciate that night that John Meagher was a good sport, and later I would painfully learn that he also had true courage as well.

On New Year's Eve, when I picked up the phone, it was Allie's cell number that was displayed. It should have been Allie's voice. I said "Baby Girl!" She was supposed to reply, "helloooooo"; that was the code we had worked out years before. It was far more intimate than merely calling her Allie, or hearing her call me Mom or Mother. It signaled a closeness that we had always felt, one never broken by teenage rebellion or anger, or disappointment, not that we didn't experience those things, just that they never got in the way of our love. As soon as I heard John's voice saying my name, I immediately knew that something terrible had happened. It was as if time itself, and reality too, had been suspended.

It should have been her calling us to check in, to tell us about their plans for New Year's Eve, to talk about the winter weather in Boston, to say how much John had enjoyed what she had given him for Christmas, anything, really, just to hear her voice on the line as one of the last memories of the year.

John said my name. Dayle. That's not much, really. But it was more than enough. I don't know if it was the fear behind the name he spoke, or merely the fact that it was his voice on the line and not hers, but I do know that my body tensed with the word. I drew in a short breath and replied, "What's wrong?"

For many mothers, a call like that on New Year's Eve from a daughter's more than boyfriend, less than fiancé, might actually be a harbinger of good news. John could have been calling to tell us that he wanted to marry our daughter and that he planned to propose to her that night. John could have been calling to say how wonderful it was that they were living together now and to let us know that he would take care of our beloved daughter, a fact we already knew. He could have been calling simply to wish us a happy new year. For so many reasons his call to us could have been a good one.

But, from deep in the darkest part of my scary places, way down deep where I store my fears and doubts and try to keep the lid on them, rose up a cold, tight fist of fear that encircled my heart and made my pulse race and my breath shallow. Only a second passed, or maybe it was a year, or a lifetime, before John answered my question.

"It's Allie. She is in the emergency room."

This was not her first time in the emergency room. I myself had taken her there when she was only eighteen months old and she was so sick I thought she was dying. When I picked her up at day care that afternoon she was already not well. She was crying nonstop and I noticed that she had small red dots on her arms and legs and even on her face. It was after five o'clock, so I had taken her to a neighborhood urgent care center, and the doctor there had sent us home with some sort of prescription ointment to treat the rash, as well as Children's Tylenol for the fever. I knew this required more than a miracle ointment to fix. But her pediatrician's office was closed and I didn't want to be one of those panic-stricken mothers who overreact to every sniffle. So I gave her the Tylenol and rubbed her with ointment and I sat in the bathroom with her for most of the night, crying and praying that she would be all right. But as the night wore on and her symptoms got worse I also knew that her life was in danger. I didn't know what was causing it; I just knew that I had to get her help. Her restless night had only created more of those red dots and with the sunrise she looked truly pathetic.

When we showed up at her pediatrician's office early the next morning he took one look at her and said we had to get to the ER immediately. There is nothing like the look of fear on a doctor's face to mobilize family and staff alike. Dr. Levine called the ER to say we were on our way and they were waiting for us at the entrance. He had already told them that her symptoms could be either from Rocky Mountain spotted fever, or other tick born diseases, or my own personal fear: leukemia. By now she was crying hysterically. The ER staff needed to prick her and poke her and take all kinds of samples from her and each needle stick was causing still more red dots and purple splotches to appear.

As the hours slowly went by, the medical staff was able to eliminate the dread diseases one by one. A blood draw or saliva swab would be followed by lab tests and doctor consultations before they would tell us that they had ruled out this disease, or that. One by one, hour-by-hour, until the only disease left was the one I had most feared, leukemia. I tortured myself with visions of those stick thin, bald-headed children at St. Jude's Hospital. By now, they had been able to give us a name for those damned red dots, petechiae (peh-TEE-kee-ay). Petechiae are pinpoint-sized red or purple dots caused by bleeding under the skin. We were literally seeing little drops of her blood just below the skin level. So many in fact that she looked polka-dotted.

The ER docs had postponed the most invasive test until they had been able to rule out the diseases that could be diagnosed or eliminated by less invasive procedures. She didn't have Rocky Mountain spotted fever. She didn't have Lyme disease. She didn't have measles and she had already had chicken pox. But we were down to the wire and still didn't know what was causing her symptoms. So the only thing left to do was a bone marrow aspiration to test for leukemia. The same procedure is also used to test for lymphoma, multiple myeloma, and anemia but if they told me that, the only word I heard was leukemia, the one that struck fear into my maternal heart. This procedure is done by inserting a very large needle directly into the back of the hipbone to withdraw the marrow from inside the bone itself. To do this meant Allie had to lie on her stomach and be very still. They weren't going to use a general anesthesia and if she were kicking and screaming as she had been doing for almost twenty-four hours, the risk of permanent injury would be greatly increased.

That is why the docs came into the waiting room and asked me if I would be willing to assist in the procedure. They thought that the sound of my voice, and my holding her was their best chance for keeping her calm enough to allow a successful harvest. They just put the question to me bluntly, would I be able to watch them insert a large needle into her back and bring out the bloody red marrow without flinching or making her more afraid.

There was no other possible answer than yes, of course, I would. Let's do it right now. And so we did. Just the ER doc, one nurse, Allie, and me, alone in a small, stifling procedure room just off the ER lobby. The lights were fiercely hot and bright, and it felt like there was no oxygen in the room. But in my best mommy voice, I talked to her, sang to her, and held her down while they tried several times before finally finding the right spot to extract the marrow. And as luck would have it, just when the doctor got that really big needle deep into her back the nurse beside me passed out. I instinctively reached out with one arm to grab her and block her fall, and held onto my baby girl with the other. The doctor couldn't stop the procedure mid-draw so he asked me if I could just hang in there a couple of more minutes. With the dead weight of the nurse on one arm, and the other securing Allie, I just kept singing and softly speaking to her until I saw that the needle was out and she was done. And then, I let go of that nurse and watched her hit the floor. I was just wrung out, depleted. Nothing more to give, and if she got hurt falling, I was sorry but it was all I could do.

While we awaited the analysis of the bone marrow, they decided to admit Allie to the hospital. She was now in a private room that was quiet and finally she slept. Hours later a hematologist on staff came by to give us the news. His name was Dr. Christ. When he walked into her room wearing his blue scrubs and a nametag that just said Christ, I burst into tears. Was this a sign, or what? Christ was now coming to tell me whether my precious child would live or die. Unbelievable!

And what he told us was that she had ITP, Idiopathic Thrombocytopenic Purpura. Idiopathic, meaning that they don't know what causes it but it often occurs in children after a viral infection. Thrombocytopenic, meaning that the blood has a lower number of platelets than normal. Hers were so low that if we had brushed her teeth and her gums had started to bleed she could have literally bled to death. Purpura, meaning purple bruises caused by the bleeding of small blood vessels under the skin, those damned red dots that look like a rash or a bruise. It was an acute case, with a rapid onset and had spread all over her body within twenty-four hours or so.

And the good news, delivered from Christ's mouth to my ears, was that it was treatable. She only had to take steroids briefly. And the really, really good news was that it wouldn't likely reoccur. The only time we would have to worry about a relapse would be if she were to become pregnant. For an eighteen month old child, that worry is so far into the future as to be almost forgettable.

Almost forgettable until the phone rings more than twenty-six years later and the voice on the other end of her cell phone is not hers. It is someone else, calling to say Allie is in a hospital emergency room, in Boston, a world away from the beach in south Alabama.

# The Birth Story of Doug Carney

A MYTHICAL BIRTH story written for Doug, who was one of Allie's first loves, and for whom she always held great affection. Now a Hollywood sound engineer, Doug was the Producer of the celebration of Allie's life two weeks after she died.

Written May 1, 2011

*Dearest Doug,*

*Tomorrow is your birthday! Happy 29th. Will and I will be celebrating with you as you add another year to your life. In honor of the occasion, I thought it is time you heard the story of your birth.*

*It may come as something of a shock, but knowing the truth may also help you understand some circumstances in your life and behaviors that until now may have seemed strange to you. They are not strange at all, when one knows your story.*

*So how to put this delicately? Let's see...*

*In the South, they might say that Meave, your mother, "got out."*

*In Hollywood, they might say, "she got all Natalie Portman."*

*In the Bible, they would call it "knowing a man."*

*In the Bronx, it would simply be said, "she got knocked up."*

*And so it was that Meave was with child. Now everyone assumed that the father of her child was none other than her husband, the man who raised you, but this is the little known part of your story that it is high time you knew.*

*You have always been told that the first time your family came to Maui was when you moved here in elementary school. Well, that's true for you, but it was not your Mother's first time on Maui. In fact she came here just over nine months before you were born. She had a big fight with your father and just hopped on a plane to have a cooling off period.*

*She befriended some Rasta types on the plane who were going to be staying in a yurt upcountry and who invited her to crash with them, which she gladly accepted. Now don't go jumping to conclusions here because those guys were too stoned to have been a suspect in any paternity suit. But they did offer to take her up to Haleakalā for sunset one night and that is where your story gets a bit complicated.*

*Meave loved the crater when she first saw it and although she told her friends that she was going to hike down into it and would be back in one hour, they were too stoned to remember what she said. When she walked away they drove off to go back to the yurt for a fresh bong.*

*Meanwhile, Meave walked and walked, so deep into the crater that she couldn't see any tourists or hear them, just the wind blowing through her hair and the warmth of the setting sun. Off in the far distance she saw a gorgeous man, who appeared to be almost golden as the late afternoon's sunrays glistened on his bare arms and abs. She thought it strange that he was only wearing a loin cloth, but that didn't keep her from approaching* him just the same. Something about his aura was very appealing to her and seemed to reel her in.

As she neared, she realized that he had a lasso in his hands and he kept casting it toward the setting sun, narrowly missing it with each toss. She watched as his muscles rippled when he circled the rope over his head and flung it toward the sun. He was hot and he was sexy and your mother was hopelessly lost the moment she first spied him from a distance.

After all, she had never seen a demigod before! Yes, Doug, as you have probably guessed, Meave had encountered none other than Maui himself, in all his resplendent glory, and she was smitten. Twitter pated. Gob smacked. Head over heels, so to speak.

As luck would have it, just as Meave's heart was racing and her breath was quickening, Maui was able to lasso the setting sun and he quickly tied his rope to a nearby piece of lava rock, thus freeing his massively strong arms for better things...if you get my drift. As he might have said, "hokeo," to secretly love.

And so you were conceived in the midst of the Haleakalā Crater on an especially long afternoon in July, twenty-nine plus years ago, the love child of a beautiful but impulsive woman and a demigod. I think, technically, this makes you a semi-demigod, but we would have to check with genealogists to be sure.

What we do know for sure is that this explains some things about you that may have seemed strange before now, including:

1.  Why you have always had strange sensations of déjà vu on Maui.
2.  Your attraction to the Haleakalā Crater.
3.  Your amazingly strong arms.
4.  Why your favorite Halloween costume is a loincloth, although it has often gotten you into trouble.
5.  Your need to have a supply of rope around at all times.
6.  Why you hate to see the sun set each day.
7.  The animal magnetism women exhibit toward you. (It's the aura.)

*I know your mother has wanted to tell you this story for a long time, but she didn't want it to go to your head. But I think you are old enough and mature enough to handle the pressure of being a semi-demi, don't you?*

*Enjoy your birthday, dear Doug, and here's to many, many more. And your real father asked me to give you this message, "Hao' oli la Hanau!"*

# The Fog of Grief

WINTERS STORM INTO south Alabama beaches with reckless abandon. Winds howl. Sand blows across the dunes blasting everything in its path—houses, cars, hair, eyes, and noses. The air can be brutally cold with the moisture clinging to the skin and refusing to let go. Dark clouds gather on the horizon. And fog rolls in so thick, with a stubborn refusal to leave; it is hard to see your own feet. And that is on a good day.

January 2, 2011, was not a good day.

In fact, it was a no good, terrible, horrible, very bad day. I had read aloud to Allie and Geoff, the story, *Alexander and the Terrible, Horrible, No Good, Very Bad Day* many times when they were children. It was a favorite. In the story the bad things that happen are things like not getting to sit by the window of the bus on the way to school, or the dentist finding a cavity, or tripping on a skateboard. Alexander thought his day was such a bad day he wanted to move to Australia, until he realized that bad things happen in Australia, too.

When the phone call came from Boston, it was still New Year's Eve, just as the sun was setting. John had just taken Allie to the Boston Medical Center because she had fainted and hit her head. She fainted because she had the flu. The emergency room doctors wanted to talk to me about her medical history to make sure she hadn't left out anything important due to her head injury. Although they were optimistic and upbeat, I read something dark and somber behind their questions. What I didn't know at the time was that her heart was only working at 15% of its capacity by the time she got there. She was already on a death track. I just knew that deep inside, the cold fear that gripped me when I nearly lost her as a toddler was back, clutching at my stomach and the back of my throat hard enough to strangle me.

I swallowed my panic and answered their questions remarkably calmly. Told them all about the ITP episode, the benign lump in her breast, her allergy to penicillin, and the chronic problem she had with one of her tonsils, which she even nicknamed Benjamin. "Benjamin is acting up again," she would say glibly, when her throat was sore. I told them about her getting Chicken Pox for her first Christmas. Gave them her blood type, which they already knew. I'm quite sure I babbled on too much, mostly trivia, but it felt like if I stopped talking they would then tell me the bad news. As in, "the good news is that your daughter is in the emergency room, and the bad news is..." I didn't want to hear what the bad news was and they didn't know enough at that moment to give it to me anyway. So I filibustered until the doctor thought he had enough information. Then they let me speak to her.

She sounded very tired and quite sick. But she believed that this was just the flu and it would pass, like all those sore throats did each time when Benjamin acted up. I offered to get on the next plane to Boston and come take care of her and she told me not to come. She and John had only been living together for a week. They were adults. They could handle the situation. It was only the flu. She was worried that she didn't have health insurance since she had just moved there from Chicago and she didn't elect the Cobra conversion. I told her not to worry about the cost, just to get well and we would deal with the money stuff later. She told me not to worry. She wouldn't even have gone to the hospital if she hadn't fainted. It was just the flu after all. It was just the flu. But they were going to admit her.

So, I did what any mature, rational mother would do under the circumstances. I sat on the sofa of the rented beach house all night long and called the hospital every hour on the hour to check on her condition. I was a complete pest to the nursing staff and they were completely kind to me. While fireworks were going off on the beach at midnight I was calling Boston to make sure they were taking very good care of my Baby Girl. The staff got so they recognized my voice and I didn't even have to tell them which patient I was calling about. I guess their other patients' families were out celebrating the end of the year and the end of the decade. We were supposed to be.

Allie's heart was weeping. I didn't even know that was possible. But it is. When the heart is under attack, as hers was by the flu virus, the heart muscle has to work harder than ever. The flu was actually replicating itself rapidly and her body was fighting back. Her heart cells were infected with flu and the vessels opened, causing the weeping. A weeping heart is a no good, terrible, horrible, very bad thing. But it is fixable.

When the heart weeps the fluid collects in the pericardial sac. As it accumulates, pressure increases on the outside of the heart, which can completely compromise its function if allowed to continue. This is called a cardiac tamponade. Allie knew about the fluid building up around her heart because she gave the doctors permission to drain it. This is how she started out New Year's Day. At 2:20 a.m. the cardiac team told me how they would insert a needle into her pericardial sac and extract the fluid that was keeping her ventricles from being able to open fully. They would give her medicine to make her comfortable and then insert the needle under her left breast under the bone. This process would allow her blood pressure to stabilize, hopefully.

It was at 2:20 a.m. on New Year's Day 2011 that the cardiologist told me that they thought she would pull through this. She was quite sick, but draining the fluid should allow her heart to rebound. She would be admitted to the Cardiac Care Unit, but after a while in the hospital she should recover. After all, she was only twenty-eight and had been in quite good health until just a day or two ago. But he did add that he thought it would be reasonable for me to come to Boston.

By 4:00 a.m. they had drained 375 ccs of fluid and the report was that she instantly felt better. A special drain was left in the heart sac so no more fluid would accumulate. Her heart rate was down and her blood pressure was up. These were all good signs.

By sunrise she was doing better still. Her color was better. She was only experiencing a little pain and a little discomfort breathing, but these were not unusual, after all a drain was sticking out of her heart. When John arrived at the hospital early that morning while I was still on the phone, I heard her giving him grief about missing the "minor heart surgery" she had during the night. But she was feeling well enough to rag on him. She still had her sense of humor. We thought we had dodged a bullet. The recovery might be slow or hard, but she would recover. She was a fighter. She was strong.

I made flight, hotel, and car reservations to go to Boston the next day. I couldn't go on January 1st because there was a band of tornadoes blocking the flight path. But I would leave early on January 2nd and be there before she would even be discharged from the hospital. Before breakfast on New Year's Day I had printed directions from Logan airport to the hospital, to the hotel, and to their apartment. I would hit the ground running and help out in any way I could until she was fully recovered. There was light at the end of this tunnel. I thought it would be okay to exhale now and get some sleep, not knowing that the light was actually the proverbial oncoming train. I merely thought it was the sun rising on a new day and a new decade.

New Year's Day was spent checking with the hospital, packing for the trip, letting close friends and family know that Allie was sick and in the hospital and coordinating arrival details with John. We had a game plan. We could fix this. By nightfall, I thought it best to go to bed early so by 9:00 p.m. I was down for the count, but I slept with my cell phone next to the bed, just in case.

Just in case happened shortly after 1:00 a.m. My phone rang. It was the hospital, the cardiologist calling to say, "your daughter was found nonresponsive this morning a few minutes ago. I need to know what the family wants us to do." I just shook my head no, no, no. This is not happening. He did not say that. We are not having that conversation. I don't know how long I silently shook my head in denial, but it was long enough that he asked me if I were still there.

"What do you mean she was found nonresponsive?" It was a stupid question, but it was all I could think of to ask.

"She was nonresponsive. Do you want us to resuscitate?"

Now I found my voice. Now I raised my voice and said, "She is only twenty-eight years old. She has her whole life ahead of her. OF COURSE we want you to use every means possible to save her. Do whatever it takes!"

He said he would call me back.

Will and I were in shock and disbelief and yet we knew we had to let Geoff, Matt, and Don and Bonny know this was happening. So more late night phone calls were made, repeating what we knew so far. We just didn't want any of them to be alone when the doctor got back to us, and we to them, and we needed to prepare them for a possible no good, terrible, horrible, very bad outcome.

Three unbearable hours later it came. "We are very sorry to inform you that, although we tried every means possible, we were unable to save her life. She died at 4:03 a.m."

I now know that trying every means possible meant that when she coded they tried: nine rounds of epinephrine, three rounds of atropine, an Intra-arterial balloon pump, transcutaneous pacing or shocking her heart with electric current, and a host of injections of medicines. For two and a half hours a total of about twenty medical staff members exhausted themselves trying to save her life and they could not.

Viruses need hosts. Without a host a virus cannot live. They breed on hosts and they feed on hosts, but they aren't supposed to kill their hosts or else they will die, too. I don't know if the flu virus Allie had didn't get that message, was stupid, or merely greedy. All I know is that it went too far. Before this no good, terrible, horrible, very bad flu virus self-destructed it would take my beloved daughter along with it. Final score: virus: 0. Allie: 0.

And I know this, Allie died in the arms of love. The staff told me that they had called John, who rushed back there as soon as it started. He never left her side. Each time she flat lined and they tried again, or while they were taking turns compressing her heart manually, he was right there, telling her how much she was loved and begging her to stay with us. His father and sister were there, too.

As the sun rose on the morning of January 2, 2011, a dense fog rolled in to south Alabama's shoreline. And I stumbled out of the beach house to go for a walk. Just a few steps from the house it, too, disappeared into the cloud cover. The fog totally enveloped me making it impossible to see what lay ahead or what was behind me. I was alone, in a state of suspended animation. It felt like my body was unattached to me somehow and I was elsewhere sort of watching it all happen. The only evidence I had that I still existed was a shrill, far-off screaming that kept jolting me back to reality. Somewhere, someone was in great distress. Someone was in total agony. I walked as fast as I could and as far as I could but that poor distressed person's cries just kept following me down the beach. I wanted that pathetic, hysterical person to just shut up and leave me in peace. I plopped down on the wet sand and put my hands over my ears to block the screaming noise. And I rocked and rocked myself on the shore while I covered my ears and sobbed.

A few minutes later another fog-walker touched me on the shoulder and asked if there was anything she could do. She said she was walking behind me and heard me screaming but I was walking so fast she couldn't catch up to me. It was at that moment that my screaming finally stopped.

And the grieving began.

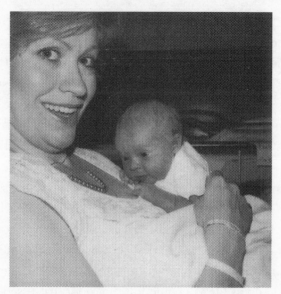

On the day she was born, Allie was alert
and curious about her new world.

Allie was a natural entertainer. My mother, Katie
Irene Taft Endfinger, found her delightful.

Dress up and make believe were her favorites.

She loved spaghetti!

At summer camp, with her friend, Dusty.

Her first sailing lesson, with Will, on a family vacation.

The world was her stage.

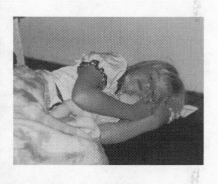

Our wedding, November 21, 1990. Emory University Campus, Atlanta, Georgia. L to R, Matthew Reed Spencer-Grice, Allison Lanier Powell, Geoffrey Taft Powell, back row, Dayle E. Spencer, and William J. Spencer.

In touch with nature on a family camping trip.

All dressed up for a performance of the
Nutcracker with Will. Christmas, 1990.

Allie's attitude was always: Go for it!

In Montmartre, France, 1993, being
sketched by a local street artist.

The Star Sisters, L to R: Christa Huseby, Nancy Miner,
Lea Flocchini, Allie and me at her Rites of Passage
Ceremony for her twelfth birthday on Blood Mountain,
Georgia. Photo courtesy of Nancy Miner.

Picture taken just moments after we both decided to cut the
symbolic cord that bound us as mother and child and accept
each other as equals. Photo courtesy of Lea Flocchini.

# The Birth Story of Liz Ambrosia

A MYTHICAL BIRTH story written for Liz, who was Allie's college classmate, San Francisco roommate, and dear friend. Liz was the "son" in their self-made family.

Written January 29, 2011

*Dear Liz,*

*You probably were waiting to hear from me last week, when you were celebrating on the day that you had always been told was your "birthday." It is time to set the record straight, honey. You are now old enough to know the truth.*

*The truth is that today is actually your birthday! Your mother, although a virtuous woman at heart, wanted everyone to think she was way cooler than she actually was, so for two weeks she went around carrying a Baby*

*Wetsalot, pretending that you had been born out of wedlock. Although it did give her reputation a boost, she did not achieve the cult status she sought. She wore a large Mexican serape to conceal her ever-expanding girth from a naive circle of friends and family. Some people are easily duped.*

*You were actually born on January 29, on a full moon night, lit with stars, under a banana tree. Your mother had to get out of town to continue the illusion. She birthed you all by herself, gnawing though the umbilical cord to free you. (This may explain your strange attraction to beef jerky.) She finally threw away the fake baby, which was beginning to emit a strange odor of urine mixed with plastic. You, beautiful and perfect, as you were, were way better than those Baby Wetsalots, with their brittle hair and painted smiles.*

*When she brought you back home, your mother always told people you were just too small for your age and some even believed it.*

*Happy, happy real birthday, dear Liz. Those of us who have always known the truth have celebrated on January 29th and we hope you will, too. This year you can legitimately have two pieces of cake and two glasses of champagne.*

# Responding in the Only Possible Way

IN THE IMMEDIATE aftermath of Allie's death, there were the necessary phone calls to her brothers, her father and stepmother, and other immediate family and friends. Each telling of the story was a new wound, a new tearing at my heart. Impossible words were coming out of my mouth about her dying that seemed to be spoken by someone else, not me.

Yes, she died of the flu.

No, there were no other problems that we know of so far.

Yes, we are having a full autopsy done and we won't know the results for a while.

No, after the autopsy is completed then the coroner has to release her body. We just have to wait.

No, we haven't decided on any arrangements yet. It is Sunday and we can't even start that process until Monday at the earliest.

Yes, we did offer to donate her organs and body parts but no, they didn't want them. Seems they don't want to expose any other people to the flu virus that killed her.

No, she didn't die alone. John was with her the entire time.

Yes, we will let you know as soon as we have any more information.

I was on my cell phone repeating these things at the same time that Will was telling people on his. Between us we told and retold the story all day long that Sunday. We would talk a while. Cry a while. Talk a while. Cry some more.

By sunset we were depleted. We went downstairs to the screened porch to watch the sunset together. The afternoon sky was fiery red, with vibrant pinks, blues, and purples. But there was one particular cloud that formed an arch from the water to the sky. It was red, tinged with gold and looked amazingly like a comet, streaking as it did, from left to right. We felt that remarkable blaze through the sky was Allie's wave goodbye. Going out full of glory in a final performance that couldn't go unnoticed was unmistakably Allie-style.

After being on the phone with the hospital staff almost every hour after her admission, I was struck by two things that happened when she died.

First, we received a phone call from one of her doctors; I believe it was Karen Sloane. She called me very soon after Allie was pronounced dead to ask if there was any particular thing that she could do for us. I so appreciated the call because it was important to me that Allie's body not be disturbed immediately after her death. I wanted her to have a period of peace and quiet, stillness in which her spirit could take its departure from the physical realm without being assaulted. I asked her to simply disconnect any equipment, close the door to her room and leave her alone for thirty minutes so she could go in peace. She assured me that this would be done.

Second, I was referred to a hospital staff member who was now the official contact. His job was to answer any questions about next steps and help me through the maze of the autopsy and the coroner's office and funeral homes, etc. But what I felt in this handoff was a change in my identity from the perspective of the Boston Medical Center.

I was no longer seen as or treated as Allie's mother, a role I had quite happily played for twenty-eight years.

Now, I had become her next-of-kin.

Next-of-kin, in the sense that, "as her next-of-kin, we will need your signature on the authorization to do an autopsy."

Next-of-kin, in the sense that, "we are sorry but we can't release the medical records to you even as the next-of-kin, without a court order."

Next-of-kin, in the sense that, "as next-of-kin, will you be the one paying for her medical treatment?"

Next-of-kin, in the sense that, "the body will be held in the hospital morgue until the coroner has finished his investigation, then the remains can be released to the next-of-kin, or a mortuary you designate."

It would be an understatement to say I bristled every time they used that term.

But we shouldered on. There were details to be attended to, decisions that had to be made. So Will and I looked at each other through our swollen, sad eyes and asked how do we give her the kind of send-off she deserved and would expect of us?

We responded in the only possible way.

We knew it would have to be a theatrical performance. It would require a grand auditorium. A first-rate production. A talented cast of performers. Lots of costumes and glitter. Song and dance. And, most of all, it must be fun.

We responded in the only possible way.

We issued a casting call the day after she died for parts in the Celebration of the Life of Allison Lanier Powell.

We responded in the only possible way.

We booked the Strand Theatre in Marietta, Georgia with its lighted marquee as the performance hall.

We responded in the only possible way.

We asked her college friend and fellow thespian, Kareem Khubchandani to direct the performance and serve as the emcee. We asked her high school sweetheart, and Hollywood sound engineer, Douglas Carney, to produce the performance and the simultaneous webcast.

We responded in the only possible way.

Will and I started writing a script outline. We asked everyone who was planning to come to please wear costumes, not funeral clothes. We even planned the party favors for each to take with them as they left the celebration. Gold bags filled with colorful sidewalk chalk, bottles of bubbles, fake moustaches, and tubes of glitter for all! On each bag was a favorite picture of Allie wearing a set of Groucho Marx glasses, with a fake nose and moustache. We felt it was sure to bring a smile, even through tears. We forbade funeral flowers or even the use of the word funeral. It was going to be a celebration! Anyone who couldn't wrap his mind around having a big blowout theatrical performance probably should stay at home. If there was one thing we knew for certain, amidst all the things we thought we knew but were proven wrong about by the death of our daughter, we knew this is what she would have wanted.

We responded in the only possible way.

Although we were still at the beach house in Fort Morgan and the Celebration was going to take place in Marietta, Georgia, where Don and Bonny lived, some three hundred miles away, we began working with them and Doug and Kareem to coordinate the caterer, the signage for the marquee, staging requirements, the playbill, the script, the acts, the after performance reception, and much more. Dr. Seuss's *Oh the Places You'll Go* was chosen by Kareem to be the theme of the performance as Allie had travelled widely and loved adventures as much as she loved Dr. Seuss. We had just twelve days from the day she died until the Celebration was scheduled to get everything done.

It would have been hard enough under any circumstances. It was never going to be easy. But having set out to spend January and February in a retreat environment, far from the maddening crowds, we were severely disadvantaged by the isolation and distances when we needed to get a show up and running in less than two weeks. Although we had our laptop and an iPad with us, the Internet service at the beach house was not working. The closest location we could find that had Internet access was twenty miles down the beach in Gulf Shores.

We found ourselves writing the obituary, then driving twenty miles to be able to hit the send button and have it go out for editing or for publishing. Then waiting in the parking lot of a business with free Wi-Fi access to receive the response. Or spending the day in that same parking lot while sending script edits back and forth to Doug and Kareem and working with Don and Bonny on menu items for the caterers.

It was never an option to simply wallow in our grief. There was too much to be done. A performance had to be presented.

And, in the midst of all the work it took to pull it off, we discovered the most amazing thing. Don called us one day with the news. His father, Allie's grandfather, John Dawson Powell, Jr., had performed at the Strand Theatre on January 14, 1928, exactly eighty-three years to the date that the Celebration was booked. What are the odds of that perfect synchronicity?

We responded in the only possible way. We wept.

# The Birth Story of Anthony Pristyak

T HE MYTHICAL BIRTH story of Anthony, who was Allie's friend from high school at Seabury Hall, and with whom she had shared the stage on many occasions. A gifted singer, Anthony is now employed with a major beauty company.

Written May 27, 2011

*Dear Anthony,*

*I'm glad we were able to reach you by phone today to serenade you for your twenty-ninth birthday! It was good to hear your voice again, especially to hear you being happy with James and your friends as you headed off to celebrate. Good for you.*

*I also wanted to write you and tell you the story of your birth. The real story. Not the cover story you have probably believed for twenty-nine years now. I have it on very good authority that this is what really happened. (I just didn't want to tell you in front of your friends.)*

*Your mother had always wanted to have a son and she wanted him to become the perfect man, not just any son would do. And, while your father was a truly great man in many, many respects, he wasn't the perfect man, so your mother naturally did what any woman would do; she looked for a sperm donor! Now she thought and thought and thought about just what sort of sperm donation she would need to produce the perfect man. And here is what she decided.*

He should be as gorgeous as Cary Grant.

He should be as talented a dancer as Fred Astaire.

He should be as irreverent as Rupert Everett.

He should be as good a singer as Pavarotti.

He should be a kind as Mr. Rogers.

And,

He should be as funny as Louis C.K.

*Of course your mother couldn't afford to go to the high end sperm donor clinics located across town, where they spend great time and effort matching the folks by educational backgrounds, religion, or financial achievements. She went instead to her local discount sperm bank, located only two blocks away, which was all she could afford anyway.*

*And, wouldn't you just know it? This particular discount sperm bank was run by a woman who was a bit of a klutz, but who had been in the Whiz Biz for a very long time. So long, in fact that she actually had cryogenically frozen sperm from none other than: Cary Grant, Fred Astaire, Rupert Everett, Pavarotti, Mr. Rogers, and Louis C.K.*

*What luck!*

*But each one was expensive and your mother would be forced to choose one aspect of the perfect man, rather than all those qualities she really, really wanted. And so it would have been the case that little Anthony Pristyak would have been born as either gorgeous, or irreverent, or kind, or funny, or a good singer or dancer, but not all of those things.*

*Some say it was a full moon night that caused it. Some say there was water spilled on the floor of the sperm bank. Some say that it was merely good luck. Others swear that once a klutz, always a klutz. But for whatever reason, when the woman from the sperm bank was showing your mother all the possible sperm donor test tubes from which she could choose (for a very reasonable price), she somehow managed to spill the entire tray of joy juice onto the floor. Those little guys were swimming into a giant smorgasbord of DNA that became a collective gene puddle.*

*Well, being the astute negotiator that she was, your mother made an offer to the sperm bank lady that she couldn't refuse. Your mother offered not to tell anyone about the big puddle if the lady would allow her to have a donation comprised of all the various sperm from all the wonderful men. It was a bit like choosing Neapolitan ice cream instead of chocolate, vanilla, or strawberry! What could the bank lady say, except yes? And so she did. Your mom got a bit of all those wonderful men's precious bodily fluids all mixed together.*

*And so, dear Anthony, you were born on May 27, 1982. And, to your mother's delight, and your father's great pride and joy, you were gorgeous, talented, wry, intellectual, kind, funny, and could sing and dance, in short, the Perfect Man!*

*Happy, happy birthday, dear Anthony. Here's to many more!*

# The Show Must Go On

THE CELEBRATION OF the Life of Allison Lanier Powell was scheduled to premier on January 14, 2011 at 2:00 p.m. at the Strand Theatre in Marietta, Georgia, with a reception immediately following. It was simultaneously webcast live. Hundreds of people gathered at the theater for the live performance, and it was seen by over a thousand more in ten countries, including Australia, Egypt, and Singapore, where friends and extended family were living. It was nothing short of amazing.

At age four or five Allie would dress up in a leftover Halloween costume and decide that she was Princess Louise Louise. She wouldn't answer if we called her anything else. We would get phone calls from the neighbors telling us that Princess Louise Louise had been there. I am sure her parades brought smiles as she vamped her way around the cul-de-sac.

Allie's first theatrical role had been in her first grade class's production of *Mother Goose's Goose is Loose*. She played the part of Mother Goose, naturally. We videotaped the production beaming with pride. She later took every opportunity to mount the stage in elementary school, whether acting or dancing, to gain the spotlight. On a family Club Med vacation, she snagged the leading role in a kind of Broadway review for middle-schoolers. While other preteens were swimming or riding horses, she was rehearsing, even on vacation. But her talent as a thespian truly developed when we moved to Maui as she started ninth grade at Seabury Hall.

Seabury is a small, private school where each student is seen as unique and encouraged to explore areas of personal interest as well as textbooks. Allie loved live performance and most afternoons and many weekends found her in rehearsal hall on the campus preparing for the next musical, drama, one act plays, or dance reviews. Although the school was over forty-five miles from our house she never minded the long days and nights she spent exploring her dreams and living her passion for all things theatrical. Seabury faculty Sally Sefton Jones, David Ward, Todd VanAmburg, and Andre Morissette became her family, too, as they taught her the craft of performing arts.

At sixteen, we gave Allie a new Volkswagen Beetle, complete with a daisy in the bud vase. She and Matt would leave our driveway before sunrise, pick up her friend and classmate Danielle Allaire by 6 a.m., drive the more than one hour to school, be in class all day with rehearsals most afternoons, and drive home in the dark for dinner and homework before starting the process anew the next day. By the time she graduated she had a substantial resume of performances to her credit.

Doug Carney, her high school boyfriend, was also a performing arts devotee. Their romance blossomed on the stage at Seabury Hall, no doubt aided by makeup and good lighting. Allie and Doug lived together one summer in their college years and famously co-parented a Jackson Chameleon they had smuggled out of Maui. Doug became a sound engineer after college and went on to great success in Hollywood where he works on many television shows, including the Grammy Awards.

It was in college where she met Kareem Khubchandani. They were both involved with experimental theater at Colgate. Kareem would go on to pursue a Ph.D. in performing arts after graduating. They were fast friends and reveled in each other's wit and joie de vivre. Kareem was possibly the only person Allie ever met who loved wearing glitter as much as she did. Allie was the first girl Kareem ever kissed, as a senior in college, and he later described it as "not so bad." They shared an apartment in Chicago and on their daily bus commutes to work would sometimes break out in song. Bette Midler's tunes were their standards. All the world was their stage.

So, it was naturally to Doug, as producer and Kareem, as director and emcee that we turned for help in pulling together the Celebration of her life. We knew that these two consummate professionals would let nothing, including their own grief; stop them from delivering just the type of glorious celebration we had envisioned.

Although we had thought of having a printed program, they upgraded it to a Playbill instead. Doug posted the casting call on Facebook and literally dozens of friends and family asked to perform. They drafted so many volunteers to do everything from ushering the audience, to passing out costumes and masks to those who showed up dressed normally. They scheduled rehearsals, even dress rehearsals, rented costumes and props. They created animated graphics, added musical accompaniment, and developed a website for the webcast performance. Doug even paid for a colleague to fly down and help in the production booth. While Doug managed the live show, his colleague managed the webcast. And, although we were working on the Celebration almost nonstop from the beach house, they also managed to keep parts of it a surprise to us as well, insisting that we be delighted along with the rest of the audience as we watched it all unfold live.

Meanwhile, back on Maui, where Allie had grown up, friends of ours from the Sheraton hotel also had a celebration in her memory. The Sheraton Maui had been a client of ours for over a decade and Will and I have enduring friendships with many of the staff and management team. The hotel is built into a hillside where one of the most sacred landmarks on Maui stands, Keka`a, or Black Rock. Black Rock is not only the western most point on Maui, but believed to be the place where souls literally make the jump from this world into the next. To commemorate Keka`a, each afternoon at sunset, a young Sheraton staff member climbs Black Rock and lights torches along its craggy path. He then faces the four cardinal directions and holds a lei aloft as he blesses the day and celebrates its end. Then he throws the lei into the water and jumps in himself and swims to shore.

Katie Brenner and Eileen Caldwell, Sheraton staff members, decided to dedicate the Keka`a ceremony in Allie's memory on January 3, 2011. Katie made a special red double lei (with twice as many flower blossoms) for the occasion. Eileen photographed the entire ceremony as Sheraton staff gathered on the beach at sunset to give her a good send off. They sent us the photographs of the ceremony and Doug was able to work that into the video montage for her Celebration, as well.

And, at Seabury Hall, faculty members dressed in costumes and filmed brief tributes, too. These faculty, including Kathy Middleton, in whose home she had spent so many nights when rehearsals ran too late to drive home, John Dependaugh, who inspired her to love Philosophy, Librarian Linda Lindsay, and Gayle Hart, Admissions, sent tributes that became part of the DVD version of the Celebration that Doug later produced.

And, in Chicago, members of her last performance group, The Filament Theatre, also staged a farewell performance. Allie had joined the Filament upon arriving in Chicago a year earlier. She was working to help put the company on solid financial ground with grants and donations. And she co-authored a remarkable play called *Choose Thine Own Adventure*. In it, she took twenty-four Shakespearean plays and made one ribald audience-interactive version where the audience got to yell out whether they wanted a tragic or comedic outcome, or whether they wanted to hear about love, or food, etc. It was staged in a bar, as many of the Bard's original performances were in bawdy courtyards, and it played to sold-out audiences for a month.

When the Filament folks learned of her death, just two weeks after she left them, they filmed a tribute of themselves eating raw leeks as a send off for Allie. She so loved the power of the playwright to force actors to do their bidding that she had reveled in adding a leek-eating scene to Choose Thine Own Adventure. Invariably, the rowdy audiences would pick it so each night the poor cast members had to eat raw leeks on stage. Six of them said their adieus to Allie while eating raw leeks and that footage also became part of the Celebration of her life.

Meanwhile, in New York and in San Francisco, thirteen girls with whom she had gone to Colgate, were rehearsing a show-stopping kick-line performance of "One," from *A Chorus Line*, as well as writing poems, and recalling memories that they later performed live on stage.

And, in Boston, her childhood friend, Melissa Schwab, who is now in medical school, was at a loss for what her contribution to the Celebration could be. She had already done enough. Melissa was kind enough to go to the morgue to see Allie while we were awaiting the autopsy and coroner's release. And in that cold, sterile place, she said the Jewish mourners' Kaddish over Allie and kissed her goodbye. But she wanted to do something at the Celebration as well. And so, she learned to play the violin in the twelve days between January 2 and January 14, 2011, because she had always told Allie she wanted to learn and Allie kept prodding her to just do it. She performed Twinkle, Twinkle Little Star, as her first recital, to a standing ovation.

My law colleagues were also part of the performance. Judge Caryl Privett, who had hosted the baby shower when I was pregnant with Allie, took the stage to tell Allie's birth story. Caryl had such an important part because she was the first performer that Kareem introduced to the audience. She had to be able to set the tone of doing her part without making this event funereal in tone. If she started crying it would only go downhill and not be the joyous Celebration we wanted. Caryl rose to the occasion, in her strong southern judge-like voice as she recounted Allie's entire birth story without shedding a single tear. Her courage and fortitude was obvious to all.

Charlie Waldrep, with whom I had gone through both college and law school, and who had known Don since second grade, was tasked with telling the story of our blended family. Charlie literally stole the show when he took the stage wearing KISS makeup. People were laughing so hard they were crying. Charlie had hired a professional makeup artist to come to his home in Birmingham before dawn that morning so that he would be able to be on the bus that brought my friends from the Birmingham Bar Association to Marietta.

All my Star Sisters were there as well. They reenacted Allie's rite of passage ceremony telling the story of her menarche and how we created the ritual that welcomed her into womanhood. Many of Allie's contemporaries were moved by this presentation and wished they could have had a similar celebration when they began their menses. One dear friend who saw it on stage asked me later to create a rite of passage when her only granddaughter achieved menarche. That story had a powerful impact on those who heard it's telling.

And Kareem, through all the many acts was not only emceeing but also busily changing costumes between each performance, taking the stage with even more glitter and sparkle each time. He also performed a lip sync to Bette Midler's song, The Rose. It was a showstopper and the audience rocked with applause when he finished. In later months I played that song hundreds of times whenever I hit a low point in the journey to recovery. Its message was the perfect thing to remind me that love is sometimes painful, but it is also beautiful. When my heart was breaking, over and over again in months to come, hearing that song gave me some thread to hold to so that I could go on. Thank God for Kareem and for Bette.

John was the last to take the stage. We didn't think he could. We so underestimated his strength. John was both devastated and exhausted. His family had flown with him to Atlanta, giving us both the chance to meet them and to thank them for all they had done for Allie and for us. Just before leaving Boston, John had been the one to go to the mortuary to pick up Allie's ashes. They were in three portions. Equal, but separate parts for Don and me. A smaller share for John. Even though he had official authorization to transport human cremains, TSA had still given him a thorough pat down as if he were carrying explosives instead of ashes when he boarded his flight. John told us he might not be able to speak at all, or he might have his father stand beside him in case he couldn't get through his remarks without help.

But when it was his turn on the program John delivered the most tender and heartbreaking account of their love story with its hilarious beginning and sad ending. He was wearing Allie's Christmas gift, a new shirt onto which she had sewn a heart on the cuff. Seems she thought he was always wearing his heart on his shirtsleeve so she was making it more obvious. His vulnerability and his great courage and strength made all of us realize why Allie had loved him so.

Will came up with the idea that to end the Celebration we should have a traditional Hawai'ian send off, by placing flowers on the water in her memory. Our friend Betty Sakamoto had flown over from Maui and arranged for 2,000 orchids to be delivered to the Strand for the finale. So, once again, theatrical magic was used to create the illusion that the stage was now water. It was lit all in blue and sounds of Israel Kamakawiwo'ole, or Iz, as he is known, singing "Somewhere Over the Rainbow/ What a Wonderful World" were played as each audience or cast member threw orchids or leis onto the stage before exiting the theater for the after performance party.

This Celebration of Allie's life would have been an extraordinary performance if that were the whole story.

But it also happened that January 14, 2011, was a record-breaking day in Georgia. A paralyzing winter storm struck the south that week causing four governors to declare States of Emergencies including Alabama and Georgia. Highways in and around Atlanta were mostly closed. The lanes that were open were completely treacherous, covered in snow and ice. And Hartsfield International Airport had cancelled more than 2,000 flights. It was gridlock. It seemed not just the state but the entire region was shut down, strangely silent and quiet.

And yet, Will and I, together with Matt, drove the more than three hundred miles from the beach house to the Strand

Theatre without incident. And yet, Geoff made the drive from Nashville safely. And yet classmates of mine from law school traveled to Marietta on a chartered bus without incident. And yet, hundreds of friends and family flew in without missing flights or being stranded. And yet, the orchids arrived from Maui, unfrozen. It seemed as if, no matter what Mother Nature could throw at all of us, we were determined to be there. It seemed as if we all knew, what Allie surely had known her entire life....

The show *must* go on.

# The Birth Story of Melanie Grossman

T HE MYTHICAL BIRTH story of Melanie, now a lawyer, with whom Allie roomed during her freshman year at Colgate.

Written February 5, 2011

*Happy birthday (on the 8th), dear girl!*

*I'm not sure if you will remember it or not, but you were born under most unusual circumstances. Your parents had long wanted a daughter, of course, and your conception was orchestrated to achieve their long-held dream. Your mother did all the usual things to ensure a daughter would be conceived, such as eating a diet consisting of only chocolate and Diet Cokes for nine months and wearing only pink spandex, with ruffles and sequins. Thus was the mood set to birth a "girly girl."*

*But something happened, perhaps it was a leap year, or el Niño, or maybe it was just a full moon, but when your head presented, it was clear to all who were present that this baby girl had a brain in her head and a few things to say about life. In fact you were born talking, not mere words like mama or dada, but paragraphs, volumes ... all this before the umbilical cord was even cut. You were heard telling the ob-gyn who delivered you to save the cord and sauté it later. How you did this with no teeth amazed some, and deeply disturbed others.*

*Now you have found your path as well as your voice. Litigation will never be the same since the "talking Grossman baby" passed the bar.*

*Happy birthday, dear Melanie, and many, many more!*

# Critical Choices

I N THE AFTERMATH of the death of someone close to us, there are a lot of critical choices that have to be made.

Cremation or burial?

Open or closed casket?

Embalm or not?

Public or private service?

Donation of organs, or not?

Religious or secular service? And so on.

In the wake of Allie's death, we made two choices that have been critical to our survival and to our mental health following such a loss.

We have chosen *not* to view her death as tragic.

We have chosen *not* to see ourselves as victims.

This path has not been without its difficulties.

In the immediate aftermath of her death, as we telephoned various family members and friends, we were struggling very hard to merely be able to recite the facts of what had just happened. It must fairly be said that we were in a state of shock as the developments had occurred so quickly. We were still very raw, very emotionally upset, and trying to make sense of the words even as we spoke them. Many, many times, our friends and family members responded in the only way they knew how, which was with their heart-felt sympathies for this terrible situation.

Most of the first expressions of condolences from our shocked friends and family members described Allie's death as tragic; such a tragedy to lose someone so young, what a tragic loss, how tragic for you. And while we appreciated their love and concern, calling her death tragic only made it harder to accept, harder to survive, and almost impossible to heal from afterwards. To be struck by tragedy is to evoke pity from those around us.

A tragedy is something terrible that befalls us, or is done to us. It is a twist of fate that seems personalized, as if we are being punished in some way and we had this coming. In my own mind, I was slowly coming to the realization that what happened actually happened to Allie. She died. Not me. When I thought about it from her perspective, and not my own, I could see that since death is a given for each one of us, although hers was unexpected and seemed sudden to me, as deaths go, it could actually be viewed as something that was good.

The death that Allie experienced was death of the body. When she died, some illusions died for me as well. I had an illusion that I could protect my children from bad things happening to them in the world. From the moment of their births, I believed that they would be safe in my arms. This irrational belief almost got me killed one day when a tornado was on a direct path for them as I was driving to their day care center to pick them up after work. The tornado was approaching them from the west as I was racing toward them from the east. I drove faster and faster believing that just by being at the day care center when the tornado stuck I would be able to shield them from it. Luckily the tornado veered away just as I screeched into the parking lot and ran into their preschool building.

I also had an illusion that things would go according to my plans. In my fantasy world, each of my children would be strong, healthy, smart, and good. They would go to college and then to graduate school. They would marry well, raise a family, and be there to take care of me in my old age. Since I had only one daughter, I assumed that she would be the primary caretaker of my affairs when I no longer could. I could envision my own demise, but not theirs. Initially, when so many people called her death tragic, I wasn't sure if it was the death of her body they meant, or the death of the dreams I held for her life and mine.

There seemed to be a big assumption that the natural order of things was that we are born, we grow up, we raise a family, and when we reach a ripe old age, our death occurs when we are surrounded by our family and loved ones. It had happened that way for my parents, and Will's parents. Wasn't that the divine order of things? Weren't we entitled to that assumption?

But what if all these illusions and assumptions were wrong? What if, viewed from a soul's perspective, Allie was only supposed to be on the earth for twenty-eight years? What if that was part of the divine plan? What if she was actually happy to be going to her next destination and not at all sad to be leaving her body behind? Was the only tragedy here that I was in too much pain to see that my own view of what was right and wrong was perhaps a selfish one?

To call Allie's death tragic, it seems to me, is to give too much power to the force of death in our life. Death is a natural, inevitable phenomenon. It is a given. Inescapable. It is as natural as birth, but by our choice of words and our projections of our feelings onto others, we label one natural event positive and the other natural event negative.

Ironically, some of the same people who used the word tragic to describe her death are the most religious people we know. The very people who should view death as merely the passageway into a better existence were the ones who made it seem so awful that Allie had gone through that door.

Her death was mere death.

Native Americans might even say she had a *good* death. She didn't suffer long. She was vibrant and healthy until the last thirty-six hours of her life. She was in love. In fact she was literally held in the arms of love as she died. John was right there with her, telling her how much he loved her as the hospital staff were working to try to revive her. Their level of love for each other was so vivid that two different hospital staff, one nurse and one doctor, both shared with me, immediately after she died, that they felt the love that was in the room. While we all die alone, essentially, she didn't die without knowing and feeling how very much she was loved.

Allie even maintained her sense of humor and her intellect until the very end. The morning after her pericardial sac was drained, I could hear her busting John's chops when he arrived at the hospital for missing her "minor heart surgery" during the night.

Our insistent belief that her death was *not* tragic allows us to keep some perspective about all that happened and still go on with our lives. It allows us to keep the pain and the loss down to manageable levels, instead of wallowing in self-pity all day, every day. We just say over and over, as often as necessary, to others, and ourselves that she had a *good* death. We were blessed to have had twenty-eight wonderful years with her. What a gift she was to the universe. What a life force she was.

And, our second critical choice was *not* to see ourselves as victims. Victimhood is a tricky thing. It evokes a certain amount of pity, and with pity comes power. The almost universal response we received when people learned of Allie's death was to pity us. Poor you, you will never see her get married. Poor you, she will never give you grandchildren. Poor you, she was on the verge of going to graduate school. Poor, poor, pitiful you. How awful it is when a parent has to bury a child.

But playing the dramatic role of victim keeps us trapped in a vicious circle of dysfunctional relationships. It is a very useful tool to manipulate others who are susceptible to guilt trips. Beyond that, it is pretty unhealthy.

All the literature I have read about being a victim suggests that to complete the circle victims need two other types of people in their lives: rescuers and persecutors. If they don't already exist, then the victim just creates them out of a kind of twisted logic. Choosing to play a victim sets up those around us to play the other parts.

Not that it wasn't tempting. My first response was to want to blame the hospital staff for the outcome.

What parent wouldn't? It must be someone's fault if a young, healthy person dies in the hospital from the flu. Right? It can't be my fault if I was thousands of miles away and didn't even know she was sick. Therefore it must be the hospital staff that weren't smart enough, quick enough, thorough enough, professional enough, educated enough, or experienced enough to cure her. How easy to fall into the trap of externalizing blame for what happened to anyone and everyone who was anywhere in the vicinity. Blame them. It is their fault that this happened to me. I'm the victim. They are the persecutors.

But then there has to be a rescuer. Maybe a trial lawyer who can sue the bastards who did this. Maybe a family member who can make the pain go away. Maybe a clergy member. Or a dear friend.

The problem with the whole victim/persecutor/rescuer dramatic dance is that the roles keep shifting.

One minute I'm the victim reeking from the stench of self-pity.

The next minute, I feel justified becoming the persecutor of anyone and everyone I believe caused this to happen to me, and I am ablaze with the wrath of vengeance!

Then, in a flash, I transform into a holier than thou rescuer, taking care of others who have suffered, too, in a smothering ooze of self-righteousness. The whole victim drama makes me want to take a bath.

No thank you.

No thank you to victimhood.

No thank you to tragic death.

Yes, please, to the Poet John Donne, who really, really understood this death business even in the 1500s, as evidenced here in his *Divine Sonnet X*.

DEATH be not proud, though some have called thee
Mighty and dreadfull, for, thou art not so,
For, those, whom thou think'st, thou dost overthrow,
Die not, poore death, nor yet canst thou kill me.
From rest and sleepe, which but thy pictures bee,
Much pleasure, then from thee, much more must flow,
And soonest our best men with thee doe goe,
Rest of their bones, and soules deliverie.
Thou art slave to Fate, Chance, kings, and desperate men,
And dost with poyson, warre, and sicknesse dwell,
And poppie, or charmes can make us sleepe as well,

And better then thy stroake; why swell'st thou then;
One short sleepe past, wee wake eternally,
And death shall be no more; death, thou shalt die.

All this is not to suggest that we don't grieve. No mental or spiritual frame we can construct would allow us to lose our beloved daughter and not be wrought with grief. We sob. We feel lost. We ache. We hurt. And we move on. We get out of bed. We take the next step. We accept that some days will simply be sad, empty ones and we live with the hope that this, too, shall pass. And some days we laugh. And sometimes we are happy. And we know that Allie would want us to dwell in the happiness of our lives together and not in the sorrow of her passing from us. We feel we honor her best when we reclaim all the joy that was in our lives during hers.

We are working very hard to get our happy back.

# The Birth Story of Sarah Stewart

A MYTHICAL BIRTH story for Sarah, world traveler and inspiration to Allie, a classmate from Colgate.

Written January 7, 2012

*Dear Sarah,*

*Thirty years and nine months ago, a beautiful young woman had a terrible dilemma. She had wanted to have a daughter for so long and now the right time had come. She could feel in her bones that this would be her year to bring forth a daughter. She was healthy, happy, and knew in her heart that this was simply right. So, what was the dilemma you might ask?*

*She was torn between wanting a daughter who was filled with sweetness and kindness and who saw the world as a magical place ... or wanting a daughter who would take the world by storm, who would travel* to its far reaches and conquer everything in her path along the way. Did she want the gentle, loving baby or the strong warrior baby?

Her answer to this dilemma would change almost daily depending on whether the moon was full (warrior baby) or if she had eaten carrots that day (gentle baby). And, when she ate carrots while watching the full moon at night she was hopelessly confused!

So, she did what any smart person would do who was facing such a dilemma. She went to see a crone.

Now some people are afraid of crones. They see only exterior appearances. They might notice that an old woman is disheveled or has a particularly large wart growing right on the tip of her nose and think, "ewwwww, she is so ugly!" Or, they might see a stooped over old woman walking with a cane that is hard of hearing and therefore yells a lot and think, "she is so mean!"

But this particular young woman was wiser than most, why else would she have been seeking the help of a crone? She knew that surface appearances are only that. One must look deeper to see the true nature of a person and not judge them so quickly or so unfairly.

So when the old crone opened the door to her small cottage and she was stooped over, walking with a cane, and she was disheveled with a really, really big wart on the end of her nose, and she yelled at the young woman who stood there, *"WHY ARE YOU KNOCKING ON MY DOOR EATING CARROTS IN THE MOONLIGHT?"*

The young woman just said politely, "Ma'am, I need your help."

And, like all crones would do, the old crone welcomed the young woman into her cottage. She gave her some cottage cheese, of course, and they talked by the firelight as the young woman described her dilemma.

"Sometimes, I want a daughter who sees the world as a magical place and who is filled with sweetness and goodness, you know, a gentle baby. And sometimes I want a daughter who is fierce and bold and who will travel everywhere and conquer everything in her path, a kind of warrior baby. And sometimes, I'm just confused about all this, especially on nights *like tonight when the moon is full and I've been eating a lot of carrots," she said. (Even as she told the old crone about her dilemma she was beginning to feel better, no doubt due to eating the cottage cheese.)*

*Well, the old crone instantly knew what the young woman meant. She was simply facing the classic pixie dust or wanderlust dilemma. The crone had seen this situation with hundreds of other young women who think that a baby is an either-or business. Either a child will be gentle, or she will be a warrior, some young mothers think, not realizing that the world isn't an either-or sort of a place, but more of a kind of both-and sort of place.*

*"WHY NOT HAVE A DAUGHTER WHO IS BOTH A WARRIOR AND GENTLE?" she bellowed. "YOU KNOW ONE CAN BE BOTH, DON'T YOU?" she added.*

*And so the young woman did just that, exactly nine months later.*

*And that, dear Sarah, is the story of how you were born into this world, as a woman who is not only kind and gentle, but filled with the fierceness of the warrior spirit as you travel the world with great courage, conquering all that lies in your path. You are the classic combination of pixie dust and wanderlust!*

*Happy, happy thirtieth birthday. Here's to many, many more.*

# Did She Know?

WHEN ALLIE WAS in the hospital I talked with her by phone a few times, and she was always upbeat, telling me not to worry. Please don't to come up to Boston. After all she had just moved there the week before and she and John were just starting the experiment of living together. Having her Mom roll into town, overreacting to a mere case of the flu, was definitely not something she wanted. Her idea was that she would be in the hospital for a day or two and then go back to their apartment and they would manage, as adults do. There was absolutely nothing in her words, or her tone with me, even after they drained her pericardial sac that made me feel that she was afraid or thought this would be fatal. So on some level I would say, no, she didn't know.

Then, on New Year's Day, the second day she was in the hospital, John realized that this wasn't going to be an easy recovery process, and he asked me to come. He needed to return to work, and the doctors thought that she might have to be in the hospital longer and would need weeks to recover from the damage the flu had done to her heart. Whether he shared this with her or not, I don't know, but based on his request, I did make a plan to go to Boston and be there while she recovered. Of course, that plan was overtaken by events...

So, when she died, if anyone had asked me, I would have said that this happened so quickly she could not possibly have known that she was dying. She was only twenty-eight, vibrant and healthy, and dying would be the last thing she would even consider as a possible outcome.

How little did I know?

Some say the parents are the last to know what is really going on in their children's lives. I had already come to this realization some years earlier when our family had what I called Amnesty Night. Having a family Amnesty Night is not for the faint of heart. It is kind of the opposite of Don't Ask, Don't Tell. It is more like tell it all in one evening, clear your conscience, and do it without any consequences. No penalty will be assessed for anything shared with the family during Amnesty Night. It all started in a hotel lobby bar.

We were going away for a family vacation when Geoff, Matt and Allie were living on the mainland, in various stages of college and young adult life. Each of them had flown into LAX to meet us and we were all spending one night at an airport hotel before heading out together for our trip. Will and I had flown over from Maui. Geoff and Matt flew down from Oregon and Allie flew in from New York.

So, while sitting around, catching up with each other's lives, the "kids" started teasing each other about secrets they knew, that if the parents knew, would really get them into trouble. Knowing what harm can be done from family secrets, I thought it would be good to just clear all the slates so no one would be subject to blackmail by anyone else.

The idea of Amnesty Night materialized instantly from a belief that it would be healthy to just dump it all out and stop worrying about it. I suppose it arose from my never having told my parents that I had been arrested once when I was in college. My sister knew, and she often threatened to tell on me thereafter. I had a perfectly good explanation for the circumstances around the arrest, but since I never told them about the arrest, they also didn't hear about the circumstances surrounding it. The net effect was that I was holding back part of myself from my parents. A little wall existed around that story that I wouldn't let them through, and it was something that kept me distant from them. I knew it was not good, but my parents were dead already and I couldn't fix that situation.

I could fix the one with my own children, however, so I proposed that each one of them take turns telling all of us anything they had on their conscience that they felt bad about. It didn't matter if it was criminal, or immoral, or merely rude. If it bothered them, and if they felt they previously had to keep it a secret from us, then tell it all tonight and we would all agree that we would not retaliate in any way, nor ever bring it up to them again.

We were taking a risk here. Every one of us was. But it felt like it was a good risk and that only stronger familial bonds would come from it. Will and I had done a similar process together years before when we had each taken an entire day to tell the other the complete story of our lives. We held back nothing. No secrets between us to eat away or undermine the bonds of our marriage. We felt that complete honesty was the best foundation, especially for a second marriage where the odds were against us from the start. Asking our children to do no less than we had done seemed like a natural progression.

But, I was absolutely astounded by all the stuff I heard about in the next couple of hours. Things that I would never have suspected or even believed that my little darlings were capable of doing came pouring out of their mouths. Things that were illegal. Things that were immoral. Things that were dangerous. Stupid. Dangerously stupid. Things that were rude. Stunning things, really. Oh-my-God-I-can't-believe-you-did-that, sort of things. Once they started it became competitive to see who could top the others' stories.

And when it was done, the air did feel lighter. They had dropped off a lot of baggage they had carried around for many years. There was much laughter. Although I no longer had a rosy, idyllic image of any of my children, I did feel that this knowing was far better than their needing to keep secrets, or pretend to be someone different from whom they really were.

And afterwards, we went off on our family vacation and had a great time together, as we did so many other times as well.

So, I really did think I knew what was going on in my children's lives. We were open with each other. We shared what was happening. We didn't need to hide behind walls.

That was why it came as such a shock to me, several weeks after Allie's death, when Doug Carney sent me a note she had written to him after seeing a psychic when they were both in college. It was in her own handwriting, complete with spelling mistakes. Allie was always an original speller.

She wrote:

*"It freaked me out to here* (sic) *the psychic talk about my health when I am 34. I never expected to live to be 34. I never wanted to grow old. I can't think of anything about being old. I've always wanted to do something amazing, something fantastic and on a world scale by my early or late twenties, and then I wanted to be assignated* [sic] *or have some incredible*

*death. Not to be morbid, but just so that I would always live in infamy—so that I would never be on the decline, my denument [sic] would never happen. I don't want to be old and bored, remen.bering things I did that were great. I want to only do great things—and never have enough time to sit back and relive them, knowing all the great stuff had passed. Is this depressing you?"*

So, I ask myself, did she know? Probably on a soul level she did. She always knew. That may explain why she seemed so intent on extracting every last drop of juice from every experience in her life. Going over the top with every performance. Knowing that all the world's a stage and being ready, willing, and able to use the theater of life to explore its many mysteries, including the mystery of her own mortality. Allie lived her life as if every single moment counted. She rose early in the morning, eager to greet the day. She was curious about everyone and everything. She wanted to go places in the world she had never been, and even go alone if no one else was up to the trek.

Apparently, from her handwritten note, she believed that she would not live to be thirty-four and so she was going to make the most of the time she had. In so many ways, she did just that. In fact, I would say that she lived more in twenty-eight years than most people live in lifetimes that last decades longer than hers did.

But then, I am admittedly biased.

What I know for certain is that her life is a role model for mine. I often ask myself, *what would Allie do?* And if the issue involves taking a risk and getting out of my comfort zone, I know the answer is that she would say go for it, Mom. And so, I do.

# The Birth Story of Vanessa Marsh

A MYTHICAL BIRTH story for Allie's high school friend, Vanessa, now a physical therapist.

Written April 22, 2011

*Dear Vanessa,*

*Did anyone ever tell you the story of your birth? I mean the real story, not the standard blah, blah, blah, contractions, water broke, yada, yada, yada, stuff. I didn't think so.*

*So settle in, grab a grandé latte and hold on to your seat. Here's what really happened...*

*Once upon a time, in an enchanted kingdom far, far away, a beautiful princess fell in love with a giant black bunny rabbit. This rabbit had fur that felt as lush as mink, rich, dark mink, so thick that if you ran your* fingers through its fur they would get lost in its velvety smoothness. Who wouldn't fall in love with such a wonderful, snuggly giant bunny rabbit? And he smelled divine! Not the usual rabbity kind of smell, but a rich, dark, chocolaty kind of bury your face in his chest and drink in the aroma type of smell ... yum!

And this giant black furry bunny rabbit loved your beautiful mother, too. And why not? She was not only beautiful but quite snuggly herself. They made such a pair and could often be seen hopping around together throughout the kingdom.

And all was well between them ... except for one thing. Each spring the giant, black, furry, yummy bunny rabbit would hop away from the beautiful princess and disappear for about a week. She would be very anxious while he was gone, worried that maybe he had been trapped by a farmer or was seeing that skinny rabbit with the powder puff tail who lived in the next village. Men are always such suckers for powder puff tails, you know.

But about a week later the giant, black, furry, fragrant, bunny would hop right back to the beautiful princess. Although he came home very tired, he always came back to her. The beautiful princess thought it a bit strange but what could she do?

What she did was fall deeply, hopelessly, passionately in love. And one spring her handsome, dark, yummy bunny rabbit brought her a giant egg painted so pretty it was a joy to behold. This egg was all pastels and sparkles and truly the largest egg the princess had ever seen. She loved it at first sight and she took it inside the palace and made a special soft bed for it in her bedroom so she could see it first thing every morning when she opened her eyes.

And one morning, twenty-nine years ago tomorrow, when the princess woke up, she saw that her beautiful egg had a small crack in the shell. She thought maybe the maids had broken it while cleaning and she was very sad to see it was cracked. She didn't know how she would ever tell the giant bunny rabbit that his precious present had been cracked. In fact, as she was thinking about what to say, or what to do about the crack in the egg, it grew bigger!

The crack spread from being slight to running almost the entire length of the egg. Oh dear me, she thought, now what will I do? (Princesses think differently than mere mortals.)

And, that beautiful egg split wide open! Inside was just the cutest little baby girl with hair that was dark black and so thick and furry it felt like mink. This baby smelled good, too. Not the usual baby pee, poop, and throw up kind of smells, either, but more like the smell of hot cocoa with marshmallows on a cold winter night yummy kind of smell.

And the princess, although quite amazed by the whole situation because she had always thought that storks delivered babies, loved that baby girl at first sight, or maybe it was at first smell.

And she decided to name her Vanessa Rose.

But wouldn't you just know it? That big, furry bunny rabbit was also delivering giant eggs to many, many other princesses! And soon the entire kingdom was filled with little princesses who smelled kind of chocolaty.

After all, he was still a rabbit.

And that's the truth!

Happy, happy birthday, Vanessa! And happy Easter, too.

# No Peace on Earth

WE PROBABLY GOT through the celebration of Allie's life on pure adrenaline. We held it together. We smiled. We nurtured her friends and John and his family. We hosted old friends for dinner afterwards. We stood in a receiving line and thanked hundreds of people who had braved the Ice Storm of the Century to be there with us. We gratefully acknowledged our family who had been so supportive of us. We paid the caterers, checked out of the inn, picked up our dog, Guinness, and now faced the drive back to Gulf Shores alone. We had paid for the use of that big party house on the beach for two months, and we thought it might be the best place to go afterwards to be still and quiet together. And so we drove from Marietta, Georgia back to Fort Morgan, Alabama, in mid-January. We just wanted to get there, close the door, turn off the phones, and stop. We wanted to go to ground.

We had survived the unimaginable. We were deeply wounded, possibly permanently broken, but still standing. We needed to rest. We needed to grieve.

We arrived at the beach house around dusk. Lugged our suitcases from the car up the four flights of stairs to the master bedroom. Put our blue box with our portion of Allie's ashes in a bedroom on the first floor. Walked Guinness and fell exhausted into bed.

We awoke the next morning to total chaos. It seems that in our absence, the good folks of Fort Morgan, Alabama and British Petroleum had decided that they would begin an intense beach cleanup process to try and remove the remaining tar and other debris left by the British Petroleum Deepwater Horizon oil spill. The spill had happened a year before and the leak had been capped for over six months, but there were still substantial amounts of tar and other debris polluting the beaches of the entire Gulf region. That catastrophe affected about sixteen thousand miles of coastline. We didn't need to have the entire beach to be happy. We would have settled for under a mile, just enough for a good walk, some fresh air and beauty.

Spring Break is one of the busiest tourist times for the Gulf and the leaders of Fort Morgan wanted to use the months prior to its start for an intensive push to clear the remaining tar balls. They had gotten BP to commit a massive amount of personnel and resources to this push, in fact it was like a military invasion of the beach, complete with battalions of workers, and legions of heavy equipment, beeping constantly, as if they were forever being backed up. The tires of their equipment were literally taller than we were, and we are not small people.

Who isn't irritated by an early morning garbage pick-up, where the garbage truck backs up to the dumpster and the high-pitched squeal of the back-up warning wakes us from a deep sleep? When it happens with a garbage truck, we can even lull ourselves back to sleep by remembering that in just a few minutes the truck will move on down the street. The BP clean up push became the equivalent of being trapped in a nightmare where the garbage truck never quite makes it to the dumpster and just keeps backing up and beeping and beeping and beeping, driving us slowly, inexorably insane.

As it happened, BP also decided to rent the beach house next door to ours as a command center. When we went downstairs for breakfast the day after we returned from Marietta, there must have been fifty people next door at a kick-off briefing. They left the sunrise meeting and someone must have said, "Gentlemen, start your engines!"

The noise began in earnest and was relentless, from dawn to dark. Now, instead of a tranquil view of the Gulf of Mexico from all the windows of the house, we were looking at dump trucks, D-10s, conveyor belts, backhoes, and hordes of people in HAZMAT suits with small hand sifters. And, since we were next to the command center, the night crew that serviced the equipment set up their operations, complete with bright spotlights, in the parking area of the house next door. So just as the constant beep, beep, beeping stopped at sunset, the rigs that needed service or repair were brought to the brightly lit repair area, just next to our dining room.

We had only wanted peace. We had gotten a war zone.

It felt that the entire sixteen thousand mile cleanup was being conducted right outside our door. We had possibly picked the worst place imaginable to recover from our great loss.

Screaming was the only sane response we could muster. We yelled at BP. We yelled at the workers. We yelled at each other. We yelled at the incredible unfairness of it all. Nothing changed.

After a few days, we couldn't take it any longer. We schlepped our bags back down the four flights of stairs, loaded Guinness and all the food and supplies we had bought for two months into our car. We were going back to Colorado to lick our wounds, as soon as the sun came up the next morning.

But that was not to be either.

On the day we were to depart, as we were debating whether to take the ferry over to New Orleans and drive back the southern route, or head back the way we had originally come, we got an early morning phone call. Suzanne Paulson, Allie's godmother, with whom I had gone to law school, was calling to say her father had just died. The funeral would be in Birmingham.

As Southerners, when someone dies, we have two responses. We show up and we bring food. Failure to do either, no matter the circumstances, would be unforgivable. I was raised to know better and to do better. Period.

Will, who had been married to me for over twenty years by this point, was well accustomed to the strange behaviors of Southerners and didn't even try to talk me out of going back to Birmingham for Suzanne's father's funeral. After all, she had just come to Marietta for us and she had been my dear friend, like a sister to me, for over thirty years. We were going to Birmingham and we would be bringing pimento cheese sandwiches to the Paulson home for their guests to enjoy. We would stay for three days, go to the funeral, and reconnect with the entire Paulson family and pay our respects.

Fortunately, we knew a dog-friendly hotel in Birmingham where they would also allow us to store the kayak that was once again mounted on the roof of our car.

No one takes a kayak to a funeral, not even in Alabama.

After three days of being with Suzanne and her family, it was time to return to our home in Colorado. We accepted the reality that no place we could go would be able to give us the sanctuary or serenity we so desperately needed. The only solution we could see was to simply go home. Get in the car, with our dog and the ashes, and drive the fifteen hundred miles back to Estes Park.

But we weren't in any shape to drive that distance after what we had been through and in the midst of the winter. Our minds wouldn't stop returning to the events of the past few weeks. I couldn't close my eyes without reliving the phone call from Boston Medical Center. "Your daughter was found nonresponsive this morning. I need to know what the family wants us to do. Do you want us to resuscitate?"

Is there a right answer to that question? Mine had been, yes; try everything you've got. But it made no difference in the end. What if I had said no? Would she have suffered less? Would she have known? Was it right to inject her with so many drugs, induce so many procedures in an attempt to save her, or save any part of her to which we could cling and call it a life?

In my own spiritual development I had come to the place of believing that it is important not to be in fear of our own death. My thinking had been greatly influenced by *The Tibetan Book of Living and Dying*. Seeing death as a great adventure, the belief is that if we can enter our own death process with a sense of wonder and awe, our soul's journey is advanced, rather than held back. I had studied it and shared its teachings widely with my friends and family. Yet, when it came to the critical moment in Allie's life when she was on the verge of death, my own fears overcame my beliefs.

I was so afraid that she might die; I was willing to have her last minutes or hours in this life be confounded by chemicals, chaos, and fear. How long did she lie there while people took turns compressing her chest? How did it feel when they inserted tubes into her groin to try to stimulate her heart muscle? I imagine a scene of total chaos, noise, and confusion. When a patient codes, hospital staff rush into the room and take extraordinary measures to help them. But surely that comes at a great price to the patient. If it pays off in success, who can argue with its trade-off? But if there was really no hope to start with, and it was all done just because of protocols, or some family member needed to feel that they had done everything possible, is it wise? Is it kind? Is it even moral?

These thoughts and more haunted our drive back to Colorado.

We made a compact. Neither of us would cry while driving. It isn't safe, you know. It is very distracting to be doing 75 mph and have an eighteen wheeler passing you doing 85 or 90 if you are crying so hard it is difficult to hold the wheel steady until they get around your car. So as we drove back we stopped often, even suddenly, to change drivers when one of us was just too emotional to carry on. We kept a box of tissues in the front of the car and when it became depleted, we bought another.

We slept, through the grace of Ambien. Our doctor had asked us if there was anything he could do to help us and Will's response was immediate: prescribe three years' worth of Ambien. He did. We both began taking it immediately. It was two and a half years later before I could sleep through the night without nightmares that invariably started with the call from Boston Medical Center. "Your daughter was found nonresponsive this morning. I need to know what the family wants us to do. Do you want us to resuscitate?" Sometimes, in my dreams, I said, "No. Let her go in peace." Other times, I said, "Do everything possible to save her."

The outcome was always the same.
She died.
Every
God
Damned
Time.

# The Birth Story of Luisa Engel

A MYTHICAL BIRTH story for Luisa, the "mother" in Allie's self-made family of college classmates who later lived together in San Francisco.

Written July 21, 2013

*Happy birthday, dear Luisa,*

*In a few hours, when Will wakes up, we will be calling to sing Happy Birthday to you. But knowing that you have begun celebrating already on the East Coast, I wanted to rise early (3:15 a.m.) to tell you the story of your birth. Maybe you are reading this as you drink a cup of coffee and enjoy the Sunday New York Times. I picture you settled into a cozy spot with a fresh bagel enjoying the advent of this thirty-first year of your life.*

*You may already know that your birth sign is Cancer and that you were born on a Wednesday, under a new moon.*

*I picture your mother telling you the story of your birth as many mothers do, with loving kindness, recounting the joy of seeing your beautiful face for the first time, or the length of your labor, or the foods she craved while carrying you. If she told you any tales about wanting pickles and ice cream please disregard them completely. They are pure bunk!*

*You, dear girl, were conceived in the dark of the night on Halloween. Your mother had spent the evening in the traditional way, going door to door extorting candy in exchange for not playing mean tricks on the neighbors. She had a bag filled with tiny Snickers, little bags of M&Ms, bite-sized Heath Bars, and mountains of candy corn. She was wearing a witch costume, complete with pointy hat, broom and large nose wart. And she plopped down under an elm tree to enjoy the treats in her Halloween bag.*

*Probably she had been warned about how eating too much candy can give you a sugar rush, or cavities, or upset your stomach, or even cause diabetes or make you gain weight. We all grow up hearing those admonitions, usually as we are about to enjoy a nice dessert. But I'm pretty certain no one had told your mother about the strange effect that green M&Ms have on a woman's libido ... or else, this story may have had a different ending.*

*What happened under the elm tree that Halloween night was that your mother polished off a few miniature candy bars and lots of candy corn and she smiled to herself and thought, this is good. Then she ripped open the first little bag of M&Ms and found to her surprise that every single one of them was green.*

*Now the odds against this happening are astronomical. The folks at Mars chocolate will tell you it's impossible unless they are specially ordered, and no one specially orders Halloween candy. So please believe me when I tell you that your birth was a miracle, against all the odds. But somehow I think you already knew that.*

*Your mom giggled when all those green, round candies fell into her palm as she shook the little bag. "Lucky for me," she thought, as she popped* the first one into her mouth. But while she waited for the tiny green treat to melt in her mouth, and not in her hands, she also felt the start of a kind of warm, tingly feeling stirring in her loins.

And so she did what any woman would do under the circumstances, she had another one. And another one. And another one. By the time she polished off the entire bag of green M&Ms your mother was fairly glowing. Her pulse had quickened. She was panting. And, she was scanning the area around the elm tree to see who else might be about on this fine Halloween evening.

And that is how she happened to lock eyes for the first time with your dad, who was innocently sitting nearby on a park bench nibbling Twizzlers under a street lamp.

Well, the rest, as they say, is history. And nine months later you were born, a beautiful baby girl, with a great fondness for candy and an irrepressible urge to eat every green M&M in the bag.

Enjoy them, dear Luisa, but do be careful about who else is around when you eat them. This could be the start of something big....

Happy Birthday!!

# Sorting and Sharing

SOON AFTER WE returned to Colorado UPS delivered twelve large moving boxes. These boxes contained Allie's things that had been shipped to us from Boston by John. Twelve large cardboard boxes to show for twenty-eight years of living life to its limits.

Will and I dragged them down to our basement and I set up a worktable in the guest room to be able to sort them and decide what to do.

We also put out an email announcement to her friends that this was happening. If they had any specific requests about particular items that they wanted to have, please let me know and I would do my best to see that they got them. I had lists of friends, mailing addresses, items they requested, all conveniently organized into a spreadsheet. Just find a name, find the item, repackage it for shipping, post it, and be done. At least that was the plan.

I hadn't counted on what would happen when I opened those twelve boxes and all the memories came flooding back, washing over me like a tsunami, sweeping my rational mind away and reducing me to a weeping pile of soggy mush, barely able to stop crying long enough to read the damned list. What was I thinking? That these were just things? Chattel? That there could be a logical approach to letting go of the last tangible vestiges of my only daughter?

Here was the cashmere sweater I had bought her at Nordstrom. There were the pearls we had given her for high school graduation. There was the ring she wore every single day. Those were the shoes she had to have even though they hurt her feet. There were the earrings that brought out the intensity of her blue eyes. There was the plumeria ring her high school boyfriend had given her as a promise ring on prom night. And on it all were little bits of glitter, such a signature Allie touch. That sparkle was her spirit, but glitter was also her favorite color.

Actually, what I hadn't counted on was the smell. When I opened that first box and the vanilla essence escaped into the air I just broke down and cried.

Deep, heaving sobbing.

Wrecking, wrenching wailing.

Falling down on the floor and rolling around crying.

Holding her down jacket to my nose and screaming so loud it scared the dog grieving.

Curling into a fetal position and sobbing till my nose was raw wailing.

Crying till I had to stop because my throat was horse and my tears were all dried up crying.

Realizing I'm on the floor of the guest bedroom like a lunatic out of control and maybe never going to get better sobbing.

Why does our sense of smell trigger such profound emotional responses? It is because our olfactory bulb is located in the limbic region of our brains. We process smells right next to where we process emotion.

There is only a short distance between the first whiff of vanilla perfume and the memory of the time the daughter who wore that fragrance ever breathed the first breath of life, or the last.

I remembered that when Allie was a little girl and I had to go away on business trips, she wanted to wear my bathrobe. It was a thick white terrycloth robe from the Ritz-Carlton. Will and I had been given matching ones as wedding presents.

I would faithfully leave my robe on her bed as I headed to the airport. I assumed that she wanted to wear it because it was so warm and it would feel like a hug. But when I asked her why, she told me it was because it smelled like me. So when she was wearing it, it was like I was still there with her. My robe smelled like Royal Secret. To her Royal Secret equaled Mother.

Her things smelled like vanilla. To me vanilla equaled Baby Girl!

I knew that the only way I could survive this process was to do it quickly. I couldn't tarry over decisions about who got what too long or I wouldn't be able to give anybody anything. The emotional cost would be too great to be endured.

Still, it took a few weeks.

Honestly, I don't know how I survived it.

I guess that one good thing that happens is that when you cry for a long time your sinuses swell and, though it becomes harder to breathe, it also becomes harder to smell.

At the end of February 2011, I packed the remaining items into a large box and shipped it to Allie's old address in San Francisco where her dear friends Patty, Liz, Luisa, Polly and Sarah were still residing. They were going to have a party, complete with Mariah Carey's Christmas music and sort the rest among themselves.

It felt like that final shipment closed one chapter, although we were still dealing with the Boston Medical Center's bureaucracy and hadn't yet received the final autopsy results.

Along with her personal effects, I sent the only words of advice I could offer these wonderful women friends of hers. I wrote at that time:

*"This has been painful beyond belief. But I would be remiss as your Big Mama, if I didn't share some of the learnings with you:*

1.  *Get flu shots.*
2.  *Elect the Cobra conversion whenever you change jobs. You can always cancel it after a month if you take a new job.*
3.  *Tell your family whether you do or do not want to be resuscitated should something terrible happen.*
4.  *If you want to be an organ donor, make the election now while you are healthy, and,*
5.  *Tell everyone you love that you love them. Don't wait. Don't let petty grievances get in the way of your happiness.*

*On that point, let me say again that I love you dearly! Thank you for being in Allie's life and in ours. She picked her friends wisely."*

# The Birth Story of Rebecca Smith

A MYTHICAL BIRTH story for Becca, who was a Colgate classmate and who became a delivery room nurse.

Written July 16, 2013

*Dearest Becca,*

*Happy birthday! Today is the day that you entered this earth, not so very long ago. You are now a strong, warrior woman, skilled and able, but when your journey began, you were just a tiny baby, new to this earth and with lots to learn. Here's the story of how you made your debut.*

*You were actually born on an assembly line, I'm sorry to say.*

*It was run by a bunch of storks who had long grown tired of all the flying around delivering babies, one at a time, to each family all over the world. Their backs were tired from delivering fat babies, their wings were* worn from all the flapping, and they were just generally fed up with hearing all the moaning and groaning associated with children being born. And, oh my, when they had to deal with multiple births, it was all they could do to get off the ground. So, these tired, weary storks got together and decided there had to be a better way.

"Let's make it efficient!" one stork croaked.

"We have to keep it sterile!" another stork groaned.

"But most of all, let's get it done by lunch!" a hungry stork added. This stork was always looking for ways to eat on the job and could usually be seen with some seeds on his chest hairs, or a bug or two tucked away for a late afternoon snack.

They were very clever storks, indeed, and soon had completed the first ever human baby delivery assembly line. Babies could simply be deposited, one after the other, onto the front of the assembly line to ride next to each other to the end of the line. No mind that the ride took nine months to complete, the assembly line was built to be comfortable and most babies didn't complain. Expectant parents would be positioned at the end of the line to catch their baby as he, or she, or they, dropped off the machinery.

The storks were happy. The parents were happy. And most babies were happy, too. After all, they didn't have anything else to compare it to, did they?

You, dear Becca, were not like most babies. When you began that long assembly line journey you thought, "this can't be right."

There were other little babies next to you on both sides. There were little babies next to those little babies, and more little babies next to those that were next to the ones next to you, and for miles and miles all your little baby eyes could see were more little baby eyes looking back at you.

For nine months, as you rode that baby-filled assembly line, you were paying close attention to everything that felt wrong to you.

"Little babies shouldn't be isolated from their parents before they are born," your little baby brain thought.

"Little babies should be in a safe, warm, cozy place to grow, not a sterile assembly line that squeaks and moans like most machinery," your little baby brain reasoned.

"Little babies should be born into the waiting arms of their mommies and daddies, not dropped off the end of a cold conveyor belt," your little baby brain observed.

And, "when I grow up, I'm going to do something about all this baby assembly line business!" your little baby mind concluded.

And that's how it happened, thirty one years ago, today, that little baby Rebecca Smith, who fell off an assembly line into the arms of her parents, decided that she would grow up to become a delivery room nurse. And she would make sure that each little baby in her care knew that it was a special baby, one of a kind, a miracle of child birth, safe, and loved.

And that is also why your families love you so much. You make their birth experience magical and unforgettable.

But, always remember, dear Becca, that the magic they feel comes from you!

With love and aloha, on your birthday, and every day.

# Sleight of Hand Tricks

E VERY GOOD MAGICIAN knows that in order to pull off a trick, she has to divert the audience's attention to something other than her hands or how she is fooling them. She uses her voice, mannerisms, or even the audience itself to deflect the focus to some other target. And so it was with me.

We began to get calls from clients almost as soon as we returned to the beach house from Marietta. We hadn't even driven back to Colorado when clients were inquiring when we might be ready or able to return to our practice. They weren't being calloused. Indeed, one client, of whom we are very fond, said she had struggled with whether to even call and ask, but it had occurred to her that getting back to work might actually help us recover.

For more than twenty years, Will and I had practiced together, often with our desks adjoining and facing each other. We worked together, traveled together, slept together being with each other almost constantly. Our consulting practice entailed going to client locations and conducting retreats to help them with strategic planning, team building, problem solving, conflict resolution, and more. Our consulting work is tailored to the client's unique circumstances. Additionally, we developed a program where clients in major transition points in their lives would come to us and spend a week figuring out their next steps. Our Maui Transitions Center program had been a vehicle whereby we helped clients face transitions like end of life, end of relationships, change of career, retirement, etc. So we were supposed to know a little bit about how to help people rise above the exact type of dilemma we were now facing.

And, given our determination not to be victims or allow ourselves to be seen as such, we decided that maybe the clients were right. It might actually help us to have something to focus on that was future oriented and structured, rather than just wallowing in the past and enduring the present.

So we said yes. In fact, we said yes to every single client assignment that came up, on the theory that keeping busy was better than sitting still.

And, that is how, less than a month after Allie died, we found ourselves conducting a retreat for a Hawai'i-based client, involving of all things, a grieving process. This client was abolishing an entire department that had existed for a long time, with well-established traditions and bonds of friendship among the employees. While they weren't being fired, merely transferred to new departments and new responsibilities, it marked a kind of death process for the affected employees. The meaning, identity, and structure of their professional lives were taken away from them. They felt terrible about it, as did the leadership of the organization. Yet, it had to be done. Before starting the new work, the company wanted to provide a retreat in which the employees could process their feelings and hopefully begin their new jobs with the right spirit. But to release the old life and embrace the new, they first had to grieve what was lost.

In an amazing twist of irony, I found myself designing a grieving process for a group of about twenty people. It required me to intellectualize the grieving process. I needed to describe the phases of grief with some distance and objectivity. To suggest specific steps the group could undertake together and alone that would allow them to deeply feel their wounds, release the feelings, and begin to heal and move on. To hold a space for them that was safe, sacred, and healthy. Of course that space could only be a circle with all of us sitting beside each other and no one having a seat that was better or worse than anyone else's. We were in this together, and together we would process what had happened to them, feel it, and hopefully forgive it and let it go.

I made it through that retreat without shedding a single tear, all the while holding them and encouraging them to shed theirs, even providing the tissues for their tears to be dried. By keeping the focus on their loss, their grief, their sadness, I was able, if only briefly, to distract them, and perhaps myself, from mine.

It was a pretty good sleight of hand trick. It worked right up until the retreat was over. And then it was time to find a new setting to practice the next trick.

Step right up, ladies and gentlemen, and children of all ages!

# The Birth Story of Kareem Khubchandani

A MYTHICAL BIRTH story for Kareem, who directed and emceed the celebration of Allie's life. Colleagues in experimental theater at Colgate, Kareem and Allie lived together briefly in Chicago. Allie was the first girl Kareem ever kissed.

Written November 25, 2012

*Dear Kareempuff,*

*Happy Birthday! Knowing that you are busily finishing your Ph.D., and preparing for your orals, this story will be short so as not to distract you too much.*

*As an Indian, you will no doubt be aware that souls sometimes return to the earth to complete their maturation process and continue their growth toward enlightenment. This has been known to Indians for many millennia. And, on occasion, Indian spiritual leaders can even recognize a reincarnated spirit as having been a former lama or swami, or even just an ordinary soul. Yours is not the story of an ordinary soul.*

*Your mother was delighted to learn that she was with child three decades ago. In fact she was thrilled. And although many women in her village experienced the usual pregnancy cravings of extra servings of curried dishes, or double helpings of cucumber yoghurt, your mother's cravings were quite different. It was not food she desired, rather makeup, lots of makeup, and really, really big hair. She would awaken early in the morning and run straight to her vanity to begin applying bright shades of eye shadow and tons of glitter. Glitter on her eyes, glittery lipstick and glittery nails on hands and feet. Then she would wrap herself and her increasingly swollen belly in a glittery sari and place her feet in jeweled slippers before she began making her hair so large it was hard to fit through the door of her house. She would back comb her hair, add tons of hairspray and create a hairstyle so big it almost made her teeter over backwards. Thus bedecked, and bedazzled, your pregnant mother would greet the day.*

*Of course the neighbors took notice. In fact quite a buzz began to develop as they speculated about what in the world had come over your mother to cause her to act in such a strange and kind of spectacular way. Finally, when the gossip had grown so much and spread so far, a swami came to your mother's village to see what was going on. This wise spiritual man knew on sight that your mother was merely carrying a reincarnated soul to its next birth. I guess swamis have seen everything, probably many lifetimes over, right? So he simply encouraged her to take care of herself and await the birth of this over the top soul. And, he added, when the baby gets here, don't get in its way, "there'll be no stopping this kid!"*

*And when she went into labor, your mother demanded to be taken to the nearest theater and placed center stage to give birth to the new baby. She insisted that the spotlight be placed on her own opening for this important opening night. The orchestra was in the pit providing soft* musical accompaniment as the labor dragged on. And, at that magical moment when you crowned and that beautiful head of yours first appeared on the stage in India, the orchestra broke into what became your theme song, "Hooray for Bollywood!" And wonder of wonder, miracle of miracles, you, dear little boy belted out the first verse and the chorus even before your birth process was complete!

And the swami, observing all of this, comforted your mother and assured her that you were in fact a reincarnated being ... the soul of Ethel Merman had been born again.

So now you know why you cannot resist dressing in drag, stealing the spotlight, and always, always being center stage.

You were born to it, not once, but twice, Kareem/Ethel. Go for it! Break a leg!

# Oh, the Places You'll Go!

A CRITICAL CHOICE we made was to have Allie's remains cremated. To be honest, we didn't cremate her entire remains because we had to make yet another critical choice. When an autopsy is conducted an election is made whether to excise and examine the brain tissue or not. Brain tissue analysis takes longer than the rest of the body for reasons I neither knew, nor understood. All I knew was that if we wanted to absolutely know what happened to her we needed to allow them to remove and test her brain, and that would mean a six week delay in the reporting process.

As a practical matter it meant that we could either delay the celebration of her life, or we could go ahead and cremate the rest of her remains, and have the service as planned, without her brain, and without her final autopsy results.

If I had been deciding for myself alone, I would have forgone the entire autopsy process. She was dead. No amount of scientific testing and tissue analysis was ever going to change that fact.

Hadn't it been bad enough? Why put her body through the ordeal? I had probably read too many Kay Scarpetta novels to be comfortable with the whole autopsy scene. Because Patricia Cornwell is such a good writer, I could vividly imagine the smells, sounds, sights, and sadness of what that would entail. I could almost throw up just thinking about it.

But I wasn't deciding for myself. An autopsy report had brought some measure of understanding and solace to Will and Matt when Connie, Will's first wife and Matt's mother, died from cancer as a young mother. They needed to understand why and how Allie had died as well. Don was fine with it. The medical staff at Boston Medical Center thought it would be helpful for them in future cases. And there was the possibility that it just might help save someone else's life. We had struck out on the organ donor business. Maybe we could do some good with the autopsy business.

And so we consented to the full autopsy, including her brain tissue.

And we cremated the rest of her remains.

I instructed the funeral home in Boston to divide the ashes into three sets of remains. One for Don and Bonny. One for us. And one for John. I was very clear about these instructions. They were given orally and also in writing.

And they got it wrong.

When John showed up to pick up the ashes there were only two sets of remains. So he called me. I called them. They had to redivide the ashes while John waited in the lobby. Finally, they got it right. John left the mortuary with three bright blue gift bags with three cardboard boxes with remains in each bag. He also left with written authorization to transport human remains, specifically authorizing him to travel out of state with them as his carry-on luggage on a plane to Marietta, Georgia.

That didn't stop TSA from treating him like a terrorist. But after some delay in checking in, he was allowed to board the plane.

John was bringing our Baby Girl back to us in a bright blue paper bag. We hadn't seen her since Thanksgiving. Blue was always a good color for her. It matched her eyes. When he and his family joined us in the lobby of the inn where we were staying in Marietta, he tenderly gave us the blue bag. I immediately carried it upstairs to our room and placed it on the fireplace mantle, with a lit candle.

I knew I couldn't slow down here. To slow down would mean to be overwhelmed by the moment. The awareness that it could come down to this; a little more than one third of her remains, minus her brain, contained in a cardboard box in a paper bag on a shelf in an inn in Marietta, Georgia. I didn't dare think about how unfair it all was. How unbelievable. How cruel. How endless. To do so would mean just lying down and never getting up again. I owed her more of a fighting spirit than that. She had no tolerance for quitters. She hated self-pity. So, I just sucked it up. Then I hurried back downstairs to sit with the Meagher family while we heard about her last few days in Boston.

John made a similar visit to Don and Bonny to deliver their blue bag.

When we left Marietta, that blue bag went with us, to the beach house, to Colorado, and finally to Maui, three months later.

Shortly after we drove back to Estes Park, we received a call from one of our Transitions clients who was in distress. He had been in Marietta, so he knew what we had been going through and felt bad to even be asking if I could work with his wife. But they were at a breaking point. It would mean giving away almost all the time I had, but they were not only clients but really good friends, too. So I said I would do it under these circumstances: his wife should pick her favorite spa, anywhere she wanted to go, and I would meet her there. We would stay for five days and let the staff pamper us by day and then we would work on the issues by night and in down times.

We did very hard work together, remembering the past, letting go, getting clear on what she really wanted, separating her past baggage from the current situation, etc. We would have our meals delivered to our rooms and work four or five hours every night.

Prior to this spa experience, I had not been able to have a massage without crying through the entire thing. It is because the process forces me to be still and quiet and gets me in touch with my feelings. During massage (and sleep) I'd been having flash backs to the night Allie died and lots of terrible pain came up for me. But my first massage at the spa was with a woman who had strong hands and did deep tissue work. She didn't ask me what I wanted. She just did her thing.

The good thing about her approach was that it was so forceful it kept me fully present and attuned to the here and now, not remembering the past. It was a wonderful massage and I felt safe in her hands because she was quite skillful. So, instead of weeping, I was just fully present in my body and in the moment.

I had my first acupuncture experience there. I was a little afraid. But the needles didn't hurt. The therapist was gifted. Such a healer. So soothing. She put about fifteen to twenty needles in me and then left me for about half an hour in a quiet, darkened room to just be. It was while I was lying there, with needles sticking out of my ears, arms, legs, etc., and with my eyes closed, that I actually saw Allie again. She was radiant and she was beautiful, and she was smiling her megawatt smile.

She was in Maui, at Black Rock. Black Rock is in Lahaina at the Sheraton and it is where they did the cliff dive ceremony in her memory when she died. Hawai'ians believe that Black Rock is where the spirit makes its journey from this life to the next and it is a place where a lot of people jump in the water to prove their braveness. Allie had actually jumped off Black Rock as a teenager, along with a bunch of her friends.

When I saw her she was on Black Rock and she literally ran to the edge and LEAPED! It was triumphant because she didn't go into the water; she just leaped up and was gone. She wasn't reluctantly leaving this world for the next; she was jubilantly, eagerly, joyously jumping from this existence to the next. And I was given the huge, humbling gift of seeing her go.

Something shifted really deeply in me in that acupuncture treatment room. I had been dreading spreading her ashes for months, but in that moment, at that epiphany, all the fear and dread went away.

I said to myself, oh. I get it. It is so simple really. I just couldn't see it before. That's the epiphany.

I knew in that moment that it was going to be okay.

Really okay.

For Will and me, the decision of where to scatter Allie's ashes was easy. It would be Maui. The place she had grown up. Allie saw herself as a Maui Girl. She loved living there. We were determined to bring her back.

And, as fate would have it, as we were working out the specifics of where precisely to spread her ashes, we happened to meet a Hawai'ian voyager named Uncle Frances Ching. Uncle Frances was one of the old school navigators who traveled across the Pacific Ocean on outrigger canoes that did not have navigational equipment. These wise Kapuna can read the waves, watch the stars, and understand bird patterns enough to sails thousands of miles between Islands just by the wisdom passed down through the ages.

Uncle Frances worked for one of our clients, Kamehameha Schools, on Oahu. As we did a retreat for his department, he and I had a chance to talk one afternoon and I told him about Allie's death and our need to figure out where to scatter her ashes. He asked me, "where do you want her to end up?" I told him Allie loved to travel and it would be great to have her end up all over the world. I told him how the theme of her Celebration of Life was Dr. Seuss's *Oh the Places You'll Go!*

"Then there is only one place for you to put her."

And he described a specific spot in the ocean, called the Road to Tahiti, which is twelve miles off shore from Lahaina, not far from Kaho'olawe where the current is so swift and the ocean is so powerful that anything that enters the water at that point could literally go anywhere in the world.

In Hawai'i, when something happens that is other worldly, or eerie, we use the expression of having chicken skin. It is the mainland equivalent of goose bumps, or goose flesh. It is when the hairs stand up on our skin and we feel a kind of preternatural chill. As Uncle Frances described the Road to Tahiti to me that afternoon on Oahu, I got chicken skin. And I knew that he had just given me the perfect answer.

This was the email I sent to family and friends following the scattering of her ashes.

*Aloha dear ones,*

*This morning dawned beautifully on Maui. Will and I arose before the sun to allow plenty of time to be centered before we began the journey to launch Allie. We are staying back in our original Maui neighborhood of Pineapple Hill in Kapalua at the home of some dear friends who live in Japan but keep a second home here. It is peaceful and still here, in marked* contrast to the beach house in *Gulf Shores* where we were when this journey started back in *January*.

Matt is also on Maui staying at the Sheraton in Ka'anapali. We picked him up at 7:30 this morning to head to the Lahaina Harbor with Allie's ashes and a bottle of her favorite champagne.

We had spent the previous day in a retreat with Kamehameha Schools learning from master navigators about sailing in the Pacific realm. One of the Kapuna (wise elders) called Uncle Frances has sailed to Hawai'i on the Discovery voyage of the famous canoe the Hokulia, which is world renowned for sailing without navigational equipment. Uncle Frances, who is seventy-five, spent several hours talking to me about his journeys and how Hawai'ians can navigate by reading the swells, watching for certain birds, using the Southern Cross, etc., rather than GPS equipment.

He knew we would be coming to Maui the next day to launch her and he asked me what we wanted to achieve. I told him we wanted her to end up literally all over the world ... Oh, the places she will go! Then he told me exactly where we should take her to insure that she would.

Based on his mana'o (advice), we told our captain to set sail for the southern end of Kaho'olawe, an uninhabited island about 11.5 miles away from Maui, just past Molokini. It took us about forty-five minutes to sail there, but it was a splendid day to be on the water. Whales were breaching. Sea turtles swam just off our starboard bow. One mother whale was teaching her new baby to breach and they gave us a spectacular show. In my mind it was the circle of life repeating itself as this new mother was showing off her baby to us in the way I had once done with Allie.

When we arrived at the spot described by Uncle Frances our captain turned off the motor and all became quiet. The currents are quite strong in this channel so the boat was being rocked while we were quiet. The water is a thousand feet deep there and with the sun shining on it, it was lit with rays of gold piercing the cobalt blue. We each said our blessings, greetings, and alohas to Allie and took turns putting her ashes into the deep blue waters, along with flowers from the leis we had received this week and a special Maile lei that was woven for us by a dear friend for this ceremony.

When Allie's ashes hit the water they immediately began a bubbling/ fizzing kind of reaction as they submerged. It looked like bubbles rising in a glass of freshly poured champagne. And the contrast of the cobalt blue water with the whiteness of the ashes and the fiery-red flowers and green Maile leaves was truly vibrantly beautiful. We took turns adding ashes, flowers, and leaves to the ocean as we said our words of goodbye.

We were placing the ashes in the water from the stern of the boat, on the starboard side. A few moments later Captain Randy told us to look over on the port side and when we did it was an ethereal, beautiful sight to behold. The flowers had been taken by the current into a kind of lineal shape on the surface of the water. But Allie's ashes were slightly submerged beneath the surface as an elongated, shimmery, white undulating shape. It was as if the beautiful flowers were leading her way to her new destination. And it also seemed that now that she was freed from her body and this earthly plane, she was so much larger than ever before. I hardly know how to find the right words to describe that moment except to say is was spectacularly beautiful!

Our captain slowly circled the area three complete times before we began the journey back to the Lahaina harbor. We brought out the champagne and drank a toast to our beautiful, beloved Allison Lanier Powell, free at last.

We will have a reception this afternoon to thank so many Maui friends who were part of her Ohana (family). This afternoon we will watch the sun set from Black Rock, and hopefully feel closure, at last, in this long journey.

With Will on a high school trip to Bavaria, 1999.

With Doug Carney at their high school graduation,
May 2000, Seabury Hall, Maui, Hawaii.

L to R: Will Spencer, Dayle Spencer, Allie, Don Powell and
Bonny Powell at Allie's college commencement, 2000.

Seabury Hall graduation ceremony. Happy
smiles for both Allie and me.

Happy to be in New Zealand.
Photo courtesy of Doug Carney.

With Geoff at a family wedding.

Allie's high school friend, Erica Keiter with her mother, Gail, and daughter, Noelle. Photo courtesy of Erica Keiter

L to R: Seabury friends Danielle Allaire, Kathy Middleton, Allie's favorite teacher, Allie and Anthony Pristyak. Photo courtesy of Danielle Allaire.

Hamming it up with Anthony Pristyak and Doug Carney

With Seabury friends, Melissa Schwab and Vanessa March in Chicago.

College graduation weekend at Colgate University, Hamilton, New York. Front Row L to R: Andrew Middleton, Sarah Stewart, Back Row: Patty Tredway, Gillian Farrell, Susanne Brooks, Allison Powell, Melanie Grossman, and Diana Heinicke.

The San Francisco girls: L to R: Patty Tredway, Liz Ambrosia, Luisa Engel, and Allie. The girls were dressed for the annual Bay to Breakers race.

The Colgate girls at a reunion in Chicago, 2010. Photo taken at the Bean. L to R: Katherine Lynn, Susanne Brooks, Luisa Engel, Sarah Stewart, Liz Ambrosia, Patty Tredway, Allie, Liza Knowles, Melanie Grossman and Diana Heinicke.

Allie, with Kareem Khubchandani and
Patty Tredway, Chicago, 2010.

Our family with Grandma Ruth Spencer,
Wailea, Maui, Hawaii, 2004.

With my dear friend, and Maui
Realtor, Betty Sakamoto.

My sister, Patricia Widmer,
with me in Hawaii, 2009.

The photo we used for the gift bags at the celebration of Allie's life, Marietta, Georgia, January 14, 2011.

The Earl Smith Strand marquee bearing the title of Allison's final curtain call at the same theatre where her grandfather performed previously, 83 years to the day.

# Happy Birthday, Baby Girl!

W*RITTEN APRIL 26, 2011*

*I know it is early, just after midnight here on Maui, but that officially makes it April 26 and your birthday. Today, if things had gone differently, you would be 29. If...such a tiny word with such immense potential. We can't let a two letter possibility keep us from celebrating this occasion, now can we?*

*I always woke you early on your birthday because I wanted to be the first to tell you happy birthday, baby girl! You would be tired, with sleepy still in your voice, but I insisted on telling and retelling you your birth story. I needed you to know how much I loved you. That you were no accident or mistake. How happy your very being made me. That you were the daughter I had always wanted.*

*Twenty-eight years of telling you things like thirteen hours of labor, being two weeks late, thinking you were a boy until you finally came out, planning to name you Douglas Lanier Powell but happily changing it to Allison, instead, how your Grandmother, Lucille Lanier Powell died when*

*I was pregnant so you became her namesake, and screaming and screaming with joy, "it's a girl! It's a girl! IT'S A GIRL!" You really made a grand entrance that day, stealing the show along with my heart.*

*Last year, for your 28th birthday, I sent you that photo album. I don't even know why I did it; maybe I felt badly that your baby book was missing a lot of detail about your early years. But somehow that project took on a life of its own and what started out to be just a picture or two ended up being an annotated photo journal of your life. You loved it and showed it to all your friends. John returned it to me and we showed it to everyone who came to pay his or her respects. It is well worn now.*

*We always celebrated your birthday, usually with a party, and once with a pony. Lots of pictures of you blowing out more and more candles and opening lots of presents. Of course your most famous birthday celebration was your twelfth, with your rites of passage ceremony. I used to say that was the single best thing I ever did as a mother, but now I'm thinking that your Celebration of Life topped it. After all, we pulled that one off under excruciatingly difficult circumstances, even you would agree.*

*This year for your birthday three theater folks in Chicago will be receiving the presents instead of you. A starving actors' fund has been established at the Filament Theatre in your name. It is not a lot of money, but it is a start and it will grow in coming years. You always felt it was unfair how hard so many actors worked and how little money, if any, they made. So today three of them will receive Allie's Gift, which may encourage them to hold onto their dreams like you always did.*

*One other good thing has been happening in your memory. I've been creating birth stories for your closest friends. So far, six of them have had birthdays already. I've tried to create something whimsical and memorable for them, like I hoped your birth story always was for you, but you have so many friends! It is almost a full-time job.*

*And I've been working really hard not to become brittle. Every single day I get out of bed. I refuse to allow myself to wallow in grief. I insist* not only on getting up, but also on taking a bath and getting dressed. One must have standards, right?

I've almost worn out the soundtrack from Bette Middler's The Rose. It is my go-to music for unslumping myself. Usually I cry right through it, but more and more lately I can hear the lyrics with fewer tears and almost believe that "when the night has been too lonely, and the road has been too long, and you think that love is only for the lucky and the strong, just remember in the spring time far beneath the winter's snow lies the seed that with the sun's love in the spring becomes the rose."

But tonight has been one of those long, lonely ones...

So, baby girl, I just wanted to be the first to tell you happy birthday. You are always, always here in my heart.

I love you.
Mom

# This, Too, Shall Pass

A T TIMES, WHEN the pain was just unbearable, I would find myself rocking back and forth mumbling the mantra, this, too, shall pass. This, too, shall pass. It became my little way of telling myself to just hold on, ride through the storm, it won't last forever. That mantra became a kind of lifeline for me, a way to keep a grip on reality when all I could think to do was run away, run away.

We did try running away.

Almost as soon as we completed the drive back to Colorado we began planning a trip to Maui. We needed to take Allie's ashes to be scattered. We needed to have some sort of ceremony or gathering there to thank all the people who were part of our lives and who loved her, too. So many of our Maui friends had reached out in various ways, we needed to respect their grief process and give them some sort of closure if we could.

We also needed to resolve the matter of a memorial for her at Seabury. In her obituary we had asked that in lieu of flowers anyone who wanted to could donate to Seabury's Performing Arts Center. To our great amazement, more than forty thousand dollars had been given in her memory. As a new building for the performing arts was being opened a naming opportunity presented itself to have a sort of permanent marker on the campus in Allie's memory. We needed to meet with folks at Seabury to resolve its placement.

And so we went to Maui in the spring of 2011. In fact we stayed there a month, in the home of one of our former neighbors, Takashi and Hisae Hisano, whose son and daughter had gone to Seabury with Allie and Matt.

We scattered her ashes. We had a reception for our Maui Ohana. We tried to be still and quiet and heal. But I had no solitude or stillness within me. I became obsessed with Maui real estate.

Our first friends on Maui from twenty years before had been our realtors, Roy and Betty Sakamoto. They sold us our first house in Kapalua and in subsequent years handled many other real estate transactions for us as well. Betty had been in Marietta, and had brought two thousand orchids for the Celebration of Allie's life. She had a daughter, too. She understood.

It was to Betty and Roy that we turned to show us property we might possibly buy if we moved back to Maui. Days and weeks were spent with Betty and me looking at houses, condos, vacant lots, any conceivable option that might allow us to live on Maui again. We would do the preliminary work and if something looked viable, bring in Will and Roy on the back end of the process.

A typical day for me started out with waking up around 4 a.m. and surfing real estate web sites to see if any new listings had come up or possibly a foreclosure or short sale that was too good to be true. By sunrise I would have mapped out a short list of things to see that looked promising. And Betty, God love her, would go along with my crazed plan, lining up showing after showing, treating me as if I were a sane person, a rational real estate client.

We made offers on a number of places. In fact, it became a kind of joke as it seemed that the only day of the week it all came together to make an offer was a Sunday, when Roy and Betty might have preferred to be doing something other than real estate. If it's Sunday, it must be time to buy a house.

We offered to buy a high-end condo that needed a complete renovation. So we dragged in contractors to give us bids on reducing it to studs and rebuilding it. But the inspector found termites so that one died on the vine.

We offered to buy a very old house on the south side of Maui. It had an estate feel about it and was a foreclosure. Again, it would have required a massive renovation but we thought if we got it for a good price it would be a great investment. But a bidding war started and we lost out on that one, too.

We offered to buy a funky house in a gated community. Apparently the owner thought more of their property than we did, so we never agreed on a price.

Betty wanted to show us just one more option. A tiny condo in Kapalua, on the golf course, furnished, turnkey. We went to see it only to humor her. After all, she had humored me for the entire month. Her suggestion was that we consider it as a transitional place to allow us an easy way to return to Maui. We could live there while we found a permanent solution and always sell it if we chose.

Our time was up. We returned to Colorado not only empty handed, but adrift.

Now what?

We had carefully followed through on every step of this process, hadn't we? We wrote the obituary, consented to the autopsy, shared the ashes, had the life celebration, dealt with the insurance company, the hospital staff, the mortuary, hosted a Maui reception, scattered the ashes, wrote the thank you notes, decided on a memorial at Seabury, set up a memorial fund at her Chicago theater company, sorted and gave away most of her possessions, crossed every t, dotted every i. Now what?

What were we supposed to do with our lives now? Now that we were the grieving parents. Now that we were never going to be the bride's family. Now that we were never going to be going to any more of her opening night performances. Now that people were tiptoeing around us so as not to make it any harder than they perceived it was already. Now that so many people looked at us with pity, unsure how to talk to us about what we were feeling or how it was going, just knowing that we were not as we had been. Now that we had lost our sense of humor. Now that we had lost our direction. Now that we had lost our reason to live, to work, to bother, to care.

This, too, shall pass.

This, too, shall pass.

The summer of 2011 back in Colorado seemed pointless. Endless. Wasted. There were books I couldn't read. Pictures on walls I couldn't bear to look at. A pool table that looked lonely and abandoned. A baby grand piano I couldn't bring myself to play. Walks in the Rocky Mountain National Park I could bear to take. Exercise equipment that gathered dust from lack of use. Friends whose company I avoided so as not to have to talk about any of it.

Mostly, we watched videos. Lots of videos. We had a massive collection of videos and a large theater in our home. But we ended up watching them in the confines of our bedroom on a small screen with the shades drawn and the doors shut. Instead of expanding to enjoy and fill the entirety of our home and all it offered, we were contracting, shrinking to exist in the smallest possible space and avoiding all areas that held memories of Allie and what we had lost.

That house was the last place we had seen Allie. That chair was the one she sat in for Thanksgiving dinner. That bed was where she slept. That picture on the wall is the last one I have of her with the family.

And summer would soon be giving way to fall and then the return of winter. Winters in the Rockies can be six months long. Even in June, at an altitude of 8,000 feet we often wore woolen clothes as a base layer. A sleeveless down vest accompanied most of our outfits as it could be easily removed for the warmest parts of the day and added for the mornings and evenings.

No part of me could abide a long, cold winter after the way the first half of 2011 had gone. Summer in that large house packed with so many memories was brutally barren. Winter winds and cold just might not be survivable.

And so, after discussing it with Will, I called Betty and said, "Call me crazy, but we'll take the tiny condo." And we packed up a few things, gave away our dog, shipped our cars, and walked out of our Colorado house not knowing when, or if, we would ever return.

This, too shall pass.

This, too shall pass.

I started to wonder where the saying, this, too shall pass, came from. I assumed it was Biblical. It isn't. A lot of traditions claim it. Ralph Keyes, the Quote Verifier author, attributes it to Sufi poets from Persia. Jewish tradition claims it. So does Turkish. It made it to American newspapers in the early 1800s.

Abraham Lincoln used it in a speech he once gave. Supposedly an ancient king asked his wise advisors to create a ring that would make him happy when he was sad and sad when he was happy. They gave him a simple ring engraved with these words. Sometimes King Solomon is said to be the king making the request. Other times, he is asked to do this by another king, and this is the advice he gives. Whatever its origin, this mantra is said to always be true, and to remind us of the impermanence of all things. No matter whether something or someone makes us happy or sad, it is passing. We are passing, too.

And so we passed from Colorado, a house with almost four thousand square feet and every conceivable luxury, to a one bedroom, 978 square foot condo, completely furnished, on a golf course, with a peek-a-boo ocean view, no pets allowed. And there we lived for almost two years.

And when they asked me how I could possibly give away my beautiful dog, Guinness, whom we had raised from a puppy and who was our constant companion, I simply said, "This, too, shall pass."

Dante's *Divine Comedy* speaks of the allegorical trip he made first through the nine circles of suffering of hell, *Inferno,* then to Purgatorio, to finally arrive in Paradiso. If the first half of 2011 marked our personal descent into hell, then the return to Maui was surely our time in purgatory, a kind of limbo in which we dwelt, sometimes hopeful, sometimes not. Sometimes broken. Sometimes mending. Never really whole.

When Will and I had first moved to Maui in the early '90s, it was a time of great excitement and joy. Our dream of living the second half of our lives deliberately was becoming a reality. We were taking the big leap of faith and relocating our children to Maui schools and refocusing our consulting practice on the Pacific Rim, instead of the US mainland. Will was able to have a boat and we spent many joyous hours on the water watching whales breach and dolphins frolic. We lived in a fabulous house in Kapalua, west Maui, in a place called Pineapple Hill. It was a beautiful, idyllic existence.

Our return to Maui from Colorado, almost twenty years later, a few months after Allie's death was a time of desperation and survival. I was absolutely certain that I couldn't face that winter in the mountains in a house engulfed in memories and pain. Will, who was also hurting, went along with my insistence on leaving, even though it meant literally walking out the door not knowing when, or if, we would ever be back. A tiny condo, completely furnished, was preferable to drifting around a large house, marked by emptiness, in spite of all that was actually in it.

I guess as I thought about it, we had taken Allie's ashes back to Maui, knowing that was where she belonged, and I needed to be there as well. Maui was her growing up place, and her jumping off place. It was her final resting place in a way, even though there was no grave and no monument. Logic said she died in Boston. My heart said her soul left this earth at Black Rock. I wanted to be near that place.

Life in the tiny golf condo was bearable. There were only two rooms, basically. The bedroom space, which included a bathroom. And the living/dining space, which included a kitchen, each was about the same size, so each was about 500 square feet or so. When either Will or I needed to have any private space, we would retreat to one or the other half of the condo to be by ourselves, closing the door on the only other person who could possibly understand what we were suffering.

We didn't know that the week we arrived would mark the start of a two-year renovation project for the condos. Each building would have its roof removed and replaced, all external surfaces painted, repaired, and refinished. And the landscaping would be redone as well. The homeowner's association had decided that our building would be the test case, the first to be remodeled. Almost as soon as we arrived, so did the work crews. Every weekday morning at 7:30 there would be workers climbing on the balcony, ripping off roof tiles and hammering new ones in their place.

The parking lot was overrun with contractors' equipment and trucks. This constant upheaval brutally reminded us of the BP beach cleanup scene we had fled from in Gulf Shores just a few months earlier.

To call it stressful is inadequate to paint the true picture of our fractured psyches. It was really a constant grinding down of our spirits. And it got worse the day I woke up with shingles covering most of my torso. The pain of shingles made every touch of my body unbearable. I couldn't stand, sit, shower, sleep, wear clothing, or walk around naked without brittle, sharp nerve endings sending razor-edged pain signals to my wearied brain. It was a hypersensitive time of emotional and physical overload, too much pain, too much noise, too many intrusions, too little sleep, and no peace.

Will and I are smart people. We have a one-week residential program on Maui, called the Maui Transitions Center, that is a kind of camp of tough love to help clients who are facing major change in their lives. We have read the literature about managing change, in fact we wrote some of it. We teach it. We champion it and we try out best to model skill sets that our clients can replicate. It was time to listen to our own advice.

We opened an office on Maui, in an old-style wooden building located under the canopy of hundred-year-old trees. We furnished it more like a home than a traditional office and our "home office" became a refuge for us to escape the chaos of the golf villa renovations. We looked forward to getting there before the contractors got to us each day. We poured ourselves into our work to avoid focusing too much on things we couldn't control. We began to focus on our diet and exercising again. We even erected a peace pole at our office with the words, May Peace Prevail on Earth written in the languages of the Hawai'ian Islands, Hawai'ian, English, Chinese, and Japanese.

And, we continued our quest for a permanent home somewhere on Maui. Once again Betty and I took to the streets and the multi-listings to see if the right home was waiting for us to find it. Once again we made offers, opened a few escrows, but never succeeded in closing the deal on any house we found.

Then we came up with the brilliant idea of building one from scratch. We bought a six and a half acre lot on a hillside in Ka'anapali that was part of a coffee farm plantation. Our intention was to build a traditional Hawai'ian style plantation house. For six months we poured ourselves into these dreams, with more passion that we had felt in a long time. We planned the layout of the house and a separate small guesthouse. We planned the landscape of the grounds, including a swimming pool. We planned the finishes, the colors, and the precise location of each building so as to maximize the views. We did everything except break ground on the construction, and in hindsight it was a good thing we didn't. Like so many attempts we had made to find peace after Allie's death, the coffee farm idea was another dead end street. It wasn't the shot we were looking for, but having it in our lives for a while allowed six more months to pass in our recovery process. It was a distraction, but ultimately not an answer.

This, too, shall pass.

# The Birth Story of Susanne Brooks

A MYTHICAL BIRTH story for Allie's college roommate, Susanne.

Written August 21, 2013

*Dearest Susanne,*

*Happy birthday! I hope you have the happiest of birthdays and that this 31st year of your life is the best ever. Here, long overdue, is your birth story.*

*You, my dear, were born under the Chinese zodiacal sign of the Dog. This may be why you have always had a strange attraction to dogs, especially breeds like, the Shih Tzu, Shar Pei, Chow Chow, Pug, Pekingese, and your very favorite, the Chinese Crested, with its hairless body and wild tufts of hair jutting out from its face and ears. For you, any* dog that was bred for Chinese nobility five hundred years ago is a thing of beauty, no matter what anyone else thinks.

But you know this already. So let me tell you the part you may not know so well. You were conceived on Thanksgiving day of 1981, when your mother, having been in the kitchen all day, smelled of the warmth of roasting turkey and your father was seduced by the wonderful fragrances wafting from the tiny oven in that little house they shared so long ago.

Now your mother was on a mission. She absolutely had to get a proper Thanksgiving dinner on the table at 6 p.m. as most of your relatives were coming and she wanted to make a good impression. But your father kept darting into the kitchen all afternoon, inhaling deeply, and then lifting a lock of hair off her neck and planting a sweet, sweet kiss on her nape.

Your mother tried her best to fend him off, slapping at his wandering hands or waving him away with her apron, but there is no stopping a man who is drunk on the aroma of roasted turkey, and probably a little wine, too. To appease his appetite(s), she offered him a pre-dinner tasting of the bird. So they sliced off a piece of the breast and nibbled it together. Well, that, as they say, was that.

No one will ever know why she offered him the breast but that one bite sent them both over the edge of ecstasy. Had she given him a leg, we might be telling an entirely different story....

But it was the aroma, combined with the tasting, combined with your mother's own hormonally charged state that finally led to a scene on the kitchen floor of that tiny, tiny house that can best only be left to the imagination.

Had that been the end of the matter, it would have been blissful. But turkey contains tryptophan, a natural sleeping aid. And your parents, scantily clad, fell into a twisted-limb, deep sleep on the kitchen floor as the clock ticked on.

They slept right through the time to take the bird out of the oven. And it wasn't until the rest of your family discovered them there that the spell was finally broken and they were awakened from their deep slumber, to a scene marked by great hoots of laughter, a burned turkey dinner, and a mad dash to pick up their scattered clothes and compose themselves.

Your parents did what anyone would do under the circumstances; they took everyone out to the local Chinese restaurant for dim sum. And as they ate the stuffed dumplings, their eyes locked with a loving glance reserved only for future parents.

And forty weeks later, dear Susanne, you entered this world with your fondness for Chinese dogs and a compulsion to never be late for family dinners.

# We Put up a Christmas Tree Yesterday

THIS EMAIL MESSAGE was sent to my Star Sisters in December of 2011, eleven months after Allie died.

*We put up a Christmas tree yesterday.*

*Those are seven words I did not expect to write this year.*

*As you all know, the year started badly and then got worse.*

*They say it takes a long time to recover from the death of a loved one. Some say you never do. I hold with a different belief. I believe that we are meant to grieve our losses and then move on. Not sure if that is recovering, or not, but I do know it is different than being in the throes of grief.*

*Being in the throes of grief is more like not being able to get out of bed, or at least not wanting to. It is eating pint after pint of ice cream and not even tasting a bite. It is sobbing uncontrollably for the least reason, or for no reason at all. It is being unable to speak of the loss without breaking down. It is looking at a picture and only seeing what is missing, rather* than what is, or was, present. It is running and running, but not being able to run far enough or fast enough to overtake reality. We have spent most of this year in the throes of grief.

But lately we have made a conscious effort to "get back our happy." We have taken time off. Gone on a trip to Napa, and Yosemite. Had really good food and wines. Stayed in wonderful hotels. Even had mud baths and massages. For the first time in a year we have slept deeply, without bad dreams.

And so we put up a Christmas tree yesterday. Filled it with a thousand lights. We even hung a wreath on the door.

We have Geoff and Matt coming home for Christmas. And we also have Patty Tredway, Allie's dear, dear friend coming, too. So we are shopping, wrapping, and shipping presents. We are planning menus and outings and gatherings galore. We are listening to Christmas carols and even singing along with our favorite ones. We couldn't muster up the energy to do Christmas cards though. I guess we can catch up on that next year, or the one after that.

We remind ourselves that we still have two sons who need us and we rally to be up for their sakes. After all, they are grieving, too. We are the parents. We are supposed to be strong for them. That's the deal, right?

And so, we put up a Christmas tree yesterday, and even a wreath. And we are resolved to make this Christmas as joyous as we possibly can. Who knows, we may even re-read The Greatest Christmas Pageant Ever, for the umpteenth time. It is part of our tradition, you know.

And just when I think we can actually pull it off, the smiling, the singing, the parties, and the being happy again ... I find little bits of glitter in the bottom of a shopping bag. Just a few pieces really, of small bits of red glitter catching the light and reflecting it back at me. And in that small moment are a thousand memories of costumes, and dance classes, and presents, and makeup and performances and so much, much more that is missing now.

And I'm right back in the throes....

I hope we don't run out of rum raisin.

We did survive that first Christmas without Allie, but we didn't make it to the end of the year 2011 without further loss.

Just as we had the New Year within our sights and almost within our grasp, I received the terrible news on December 29th that my older sister, Patricia, whom we always called Pat, had died.

Pat's death can't be said to have been a surprise, but it certainly was a blow. She was seventy years old and had been in liver failure for several years. Although she was on an organ transplant list she knew she was too old to receive one.

Pat was what would be called a "good Mormon." That was part of the irony of her death. Someone whom had never even tasted alcohol developed cirrhosis of the liver. It just seemed so unfair.

Pat had left our home in Alabama when she was eighteen to marry a Mormon guy she met while in high school. I was only nine when she boarded that Greyhound Bus for Utah. I remember the day she left. It felt like she died then because we didn't see her again for years and she didn't write much. I was a teenager before I next saw her and she was a mother.

The distance of my early life in the Deep South and her young adulthood in Utah kept us apart for a long time. But when we moved to Colorado Will and I were able to reconnect with Pat and Bruce and their entire brood.

And she came to see me right before we moved from Colorado back to Maui. It required tremendous effort for her to make that trip, as she was pretty weak by then. I remember the shock I felt when I met their flight at the Denver airport. She looked so swollen and tired. I think we both knew it would be our last time to be together.

When she died, Bruce asked me to deliver the eulogy at her funeral. I was deeply honored to do so.

And that's how I came to spend the first anniversary of Allie's death on a red-eye flight from Maui to Salt Lake. I probably wouldn't have been able to sleep that night anyway. But spending it at 30,000 feet while writing Pat's eulogy gave new depths to the meaning of grief and loss.

On the very day that I felt most in need of being comforted, when all my bad memories of that no good, terrible, horrible very bad day came washing back to my consciousness, I was being asked to give comfort to Pat's family. Bruce must have seen some strength in me that I didn't know I had.

I was not sorry to see the end of 2011.

But Pat's death wasn't the last of our woes. I had just returned from her funeral when we got the word that Will's wonderful mother, Ruth Van Cleave Spencer, died peacefully on January 11, 2012. I was still spinning from the anniversary of Allie's death, my sister's death and funeral, and was now facing yet another big loss.

Ruth was ninety-six years old and no one could have been surprised by her death. She had a belly riddled with cancer so it wasn't a matter of whether, but when, she would die. Yet this woman had already beaten brain cancer years before so in some ways she seemed invincible.

That was certainly the case when she showed up as a surprise at the grand opening of our offices on Maui in the fall of 2011, just three months before she died. Ruth was one of those strong, mid-western women, who had true grit. And that's exactly what it took for her to be able to make the flight from Los Angeles, California to Maui to pull off one of the happiest surprises of my life.

Will and I had planned a big party celebration for our office opening. The Governor of Hawaii, Neil Abercrombie, had sent an emissary and his personal greetings, as had the Mayor of Maui County, Alan Arakawa. Our state legislator, Senator Roz Baker, was there for the ribbon cutting. We had live music, catering on the big lawn behind our office and of course, leis and hula dancers to set the Hawai'ian style mood for the party. Many friends and clients were coming, but so far as we knew no one from our families would be able to be there. It was all set to begin just before sunset.

And around 4pm, I heard a car pulling up to our office door. Assuming it was the caterers, I went to open the door and saw instead that it was my Brother and Sister in Law, John and Susan Camphouse, Will's sister and her husband. That was such a delight and a thrill to see that they had traveled so far to surprise us. But as John got out of the driver's side of the car, he opened the back door and there was Ruth, grinning like the Cheshire cat!

I literally started shrieking, Oh My God! Oh My God!!!! Will heard the commotion and came to the door about the time that I started crying from sheer joy. And his frail, wonderful mother slowly made her way up our wheelchair ramp to see for herself what this new chapter of our lives would be like. We simply couldn't believe that she was able to make the journey or that she would even try. Yet, there she was, regal, inquisitive, and ever attentive to what was happening in our lives.

When Allie died, Ruth had told me that she didn't even know what to say to us to console us. She was never supposed to live long enough to see the death of one of her grandchildren, she said. She felt totally inadequate to the task. Whatever she might have said to us in our saddened state of grief at that time probably wouldn't have made much of a dent. But the act of getting on that plane, although she was in tremendous pain and weakened by the spread of the cancer throughout her abdomen, was such an inspiration to me that she lifted my sodden spirits immeasurably.

Along with Susie and John, their son David and his family, and their daughter Debbie, and her family was also part of the big surprise. Our office opening became a kind of Spencer family reunion, to our great delight. A weekend filled with family meals, laughter, and good times followed our party. Three months later, my sister and my mother in law were both dead.

Yet Ruth had a good death. In fact, I would say it was a very good death. She deserved it. She was the daughter of an old-school physician, one who made his house calls in with a horse and buggy that Ruth sometimes drove. She loved sciences, especially medical science and she was very pragmatic about disease, even when it was her own. She lived independently, in her own home, with the assistance of Susie and John, paying her own bills, and driving her own car until shortly before she died. She knew she had metastasized cancer and renal failure. She chose not to go into a nursing home or hospital, rather to stay in her own bed until the end.

Ruth's death was a kind of reverse birth process, with Susie playing the role of the caring mid-wife. Susie, and hospice workers, were with her around the clock as the end approached. And Susie literally climbed into the bed with her mother, holding her and gently rocking her frail body as Ruth took her last breaths. Ruth's beloved dog, Pepper, was in that bed as well. It was a beautiful death, calm and peaceful. A simple letting go. A surrender.

With Pat's death, and Ruth's coming so closely on the heels of Allie's I experienced a kind of denial about their passing. It was as if I simply put my emotional response to their deaths in some sort of remote parking lot, a distance away from my feelings and heart space. I knew they were dead. I was there for the funerals. Went through all the motions of the endings, but at an emotional distance. I know that therapists call this sort of piling on Compounded Grief. Grief for one family member would be enough. But finding the emotional wellspring that would allow me to grieve for all three simultaneously just wasn't possible for me.

As much as Allie loved William Shakespeare, it was starting to feel like we were caught up in one of his plays, with tragedy behind every door. As the bard himself put it, in Hamlet, *"When sorrows come, they come not single spies, (b)ut in battalions."* Ruth's death, although gentle, and perhaps even perfect, was our third time at bat in the space of a year. We had struck out each time.

# The Birth Story of Melissa Schwab

A MYTHICAL BIRTH story for Allie's high school friend, Melissa, now in medical school. When Melissa learned of Allie's death she went to the morgue in Boston to say the mourner's Kaddish over her body. She also learned to play the violin in two weeks so she could perform in the celebration of Allie's life.

Written December 12, 2012

*Happy Birthday, dear Melissa!*

*I've been meaning to tell you your birth story for some time now, but it always seems that I get caught up with the demands of the season each December and miss the window of opportunity. I'll bet you hate when retailers overtake your special day year after year! Being a December baby has its challenges.*

*One of its rewards, however, is being a Sagittarius. Your birth symbol is the archer, with the bow drawn and the arrow pointing toward its target. You, Melissa, have always been the one with your eyes focused on the target ahead and your arrow heading straight toward its mark. There is no stopping you once your mind is made up, you are the veritable force to be reckoned with by the rest of the world. And that laser-like focus is how you entered this world, three decades ago.*

*While most babies spend their time in utero just floating around, sleeping, waiting and growing, you were busy planning your entry strategy. Not one to swim around all day sucking your little baby thumb, you managed to whittle a tiny little arrow from the debris you collected from the amniotic sac. Wendy felt this baby arrow as a sharp pang, and promptly reported it to her doctor, who told her not worry, just have another kosher pickle and wait it out.*

*While she waited, you grew, and so did the little arrow as you continued your work on it. Wendy's pangs grew sharper and her complaints grew louder, but the clueless doctor just patted her shoulder and said he would see her again in a couple of weeks. As your pregnancy went by, these stabbing pangs became commonplace. Not having been pregnant before, Wendy came to accept them as normal. You began to think you needed a larger space to work and you were tired of being bent over.*

*Now Sagittarians are quite competitive, even as babies, and you were no exception to this rule. So on the day when Wendy's doctor was explaining to her that first labors can be quite lengthy and sometimes difficult, you began to think of a better way to be born than he was planning for you. And a few weeks later, when she was in the doctor's office having yet another check up, you executed your well-crafted plan.*

*The nurse had just gotten Wendy settled into the stirrups of the examination table with her feet high in the air and her legs bent as she lay on her back. And the doctor was just putting that jelly stuff on his examination glove when you took aim with your arrow and shot your mark just over his shoulder at a target-shaped drawing, hitting it dead center, of course. Once your arrow was in place, you just climbed right out of the womb, landing in the extremely excited doctor's slippery hands.*

*When your mother saw the arrow, she understood what all those sharp pangs had been about, and that this baby would go far in life, letting neither the ignorance nor inexperience of those around her keep her from making her targeted goals.*

*And you, dear Melissa, have been hitting the mark ever since, whether it was being first in your class, getting into medical school, or learning the violin in just two weeks, you have set your bow aim high and shot each arrow strong and true.*

*Happy, happy birthday, dear girl. And many more!*

# My Mother. My Daughter. Myself.

M Y MOTHER GAVE birth to ten children. I was the eighth. She had six daughters. I was the fifth girl born. She claimed she raised all of us on only one dozen diapers and had us potty trained by the time we could walk. I always had trouble believing that one.

She breast-fed all of us. Many were born at home. For most of her life she had only an eighth grade education. But when she was seventy-two and finally free of responsibility for her large family, she went back to high school and graduated. I was there for her commencement. I have never been more proud to be her daughter than that day.

She cooked three hot meals a day for sixty-five years of her married life and made biscuits from scratch for most of them. She married my father when she was only fifteen and became a mother when she was seventeen.

She lost a daughter, too. In fact it was her first child. My sister Bobby Dean died at birth. The pregnancy was pretty risky. So much so that the doctor advised my mother not to have any more children. She only had nine others. I remember the absence of Bobby Dean, as if I had known her. We grew up saying things like, "if Bobby Dean were alive today, she'd be ___ years old." If Bobby Dean were actually alive today she'd be over eighty.

All my life I wondered why my parents had never practiced birth control. There were too many of us and too little money. No one would have intentionally created so many mouths to feed when there was so little food to go around. And, when I was an adult, Mother told me they actually had used birth control. They practiced the rhythm method. I never remember seeing my parents dancing and I guess the reason is obvious.

My mother was badly injured as a little girl. She was about two years old and was rocking by the fireplace in her family's home when her rocking chair tipped over, tossing her little body into the fire. She lost the fingers on her right hand and her thumb was also badly burned. She had been right handed, but had to learn to do everything left-handed. She was always embarrassed by her hand, especially when meeting new people. I never thought of her as handicapped. After all she raised all those children. She even drove a car. A stick shift.

My mother had always wanted to be a nurse. Her aunt was a nurse and she'd had a good life. She had many pretty things. When she died my mother inherited some of them. My mother never became a nurse, but she nursed all my childhood hurts. She also pulled my teeth. Nothing seemed to please her so much as a kid with a loose tooth. She would tie a string to the tooth and tie the other end around a doorknob and slam that door as hard as she could. The tooth would pop out, to be placed under our pillows for a visit by the tooth fairy. In our house the tooth fairy was poor too. We would get a nickel or maybe a dime.

Although they had nine months to think about it, my mother and father didn't name me. I suppose maybe they had used up all the good names by the time I came along. By then they had gone through fourteen names. They let the nurse at the hospital where I was born give me my name. She had always wanted a daughter and if she had one she would have named her Burma Dayle. I really wish that nurse had gotten her wish and some other little girl had been given my name. I hated that name so much that when I started law school I legally changed it, dropping the Burma bit forever.

Technically, my mother lived to be eighty-six. In reality, dementia took the mother I knew and loved years before she stopped eating long enough to starve to death. One of the worst days of my life was the day my mother didn't recognize me. She said I looked familiar but she couldn't place me. Was I one of the nurses at the nursing home who took care of her? I said, through tears, "No ma'am. It's me, Momma. Dayle. I'm your daughter." No daughter should ever have to tell her mother that.

My mother was Katie Irene Taft Endfinger. She was born in Talladega, Alabama. She lived in Alabama her entire life. She left the mainland once, to come visit me in Hawaii. Her nine children produced twenty-three grand children, and even more great grand children.

In her last days, my sister Ann cared for my mother in her mobile home in Selma, Alabama. She died there under hospice care not long after she stopped eating. I flew home from Maui but couldn't get there before she was gone.

Ever since that day I have wanted to write a new country-western song. It's haunting me, but I don't have all the lyrics worked out yet. I am sure of the title, though, and I think it will be an instant hit. "My Mamma Died In a Double Wide."

My daughter was born on April 26, 1982, at St. Vincent's Hospital in Birmingham, Alabama. She was a delight and amazement to me from her first breath of life. When she surprised us all by being a girl, I started screaming, Baby Girl! Baby Girl! Baby Girl!!!! I called her that the rest of her life.

My mother came to the hospital to meet her granddaughter when she was born. I have pictures of them together. My mother had brown eyes. My daughter's eyes were blue. My mother had brown hair. My daughter's hair was blonde.

My daughter got chicken pox her first Christmas, when she was only eight months old. My mother said not to worry. It was good to get those things out of the way while they were young. My mother had seen to it that all her children got their share of measles, mumps, and chicken pox while growing up. My daughter had been given immunizations to protect her from childhood diseases.

My daughter had a bedroom fit for a princess with a canopied bed with frilly pink and green bedding. She had a collection of stuffed animals that could have filled a zoo. She took ballet, tap, and jazz and had an entire wardrobe of costumes for her dance classes. She had birthday parties and sleepovers and at age eight was escorted to the Nutcracker suite by her stepfather in a tuxedo while she wore a long dress.

My daughter was in the gifted program from elementary school on. She graduated with honors from high school and college. My daughter went to private schools on Maui and in New York. We took her to Broadway plays. She was the president of the student body at her high school. She was a member of a sorority in college until she decided she was over it.

My daughter had moved from Alabama to Georgia to Maui by high school. Then went to New York, Scotland, Australia, France, England, and the Netherlands before finishing college. She lived in San Francisco, Melbourne, Chicago, and finally, Boston, too.

She fell in love, more than once, but never married.

She was in theatrical performances from the time she was five until the week she died. She acted, wrote, directed, produced, made costumes, raised money, sold tickets, and lived for opening nights. She loved the Bay to Breakers race in San Francisco and worked feverishly to dress all her friends in costumes to be part of the fun. One year they all went as tacos.

And when she died, I learned from the autopsy report that she had an IUD. It shouldn't have been surprising because she clearly didn't want to have children at that point in her life. In fact she once told me she would never have children. I guess I had just thought that we might have discussed it if she was getting an IUD. A mother should not have to learn this from an autopsy.

My daughter loved the movie *Princess Bride*. She owned it. I gave it to her. We watched it together so many times I can say the lines by heart. She also loved Mariah Carey's Christmas album. I gave her that, too. We knew the words to every single song. We would sing it together as if no one was listening, even when it wasn't Christmas. My daughter couldn't carry a tune, but that didn't stop her from singing.

My daughter made the most fantastic greeting cards. They were all by hand, very creative, and so thoughtful. When her dear friend turned seventeen she made a card listing seventeen reasons to love Melissa. She was an original, one of a kind.

And now, when I miss my mother and my daughter more than I can bear, I have a little music box by my bed that has a picture of them taken when my daughter was just a girl. She is being held by my mother and is making a terrible face at her. My mother is laughing so hard at my daughter, the imp. The music box plays the tune *Memories*. And I'm left with these memories and many more, and the music of Andrew Lloyd Webber to help me cope.

# The Birth Story of Erica Keiter

A NON-MYTHICAL BIRTH story for one of Allie's first friends on Maui, whose mother, like Allie, died too soon.

Written March 12, 2013

*Dearest Erica,*

*Happy birthday, honey!*
*I've been struggling to write your birth story for quite a while. I wanted to write one that was mythical, playful, even funny, but somehow I can't force those words out of my mouth, or onto the paper. Our relationship has been too intense, too personal for me to be able to capture its meaning with farce.*

*After all, who among Allie's closest friends calls me Mother Sheraton, but you?*

*You and I share a special, terrible bond. You lost your mother, too soon, and I lost my daughter as well. The relationship that Gail, Allie, and you and I shared as mothers/daughters was unique. You were a part of our family and we were a part of yours. That was true almost from the first day you two girls met on the beach at Napili Kai when we washed up on Maui.*

*As I think about your birth story, Erica, in spite of biological evidence to the contrary, I think you actually gave birth to Gail, and not the other way around. In so many ways your arrival completed Gail's life and satisfied some deep longing in her to truly know who she was and what she was meant to be in this world.*

*As you know, having been adopted she struggled with her sense of belonging and needing to feel love. You came into this world as a joyous bundle of love, with laughter and acceptance of everyone. Your life force was just the thing to show Gail that she was worthy of love. She basked in your ease of meeting new friends and your popularity. I'm sure that your radiant smile warmed the dark places in her heart where she was afraid. Gail was proud of you and proud and happy to be your mother.*

*I got a real sense of the depth of her pride when you were a high school cheerleader and I sat next to her at a Lahainaluna football game and watched her watch you move the crowds to excitement and cheer the team on to victory. Every jump you made, every pom pom you waved, she watched and admired.*

*You gave her the great gift of reflection as the resemblance you bear to her showed her that she, too, could be beautiful, happy, and loved. And in many ways, your early maturity was a stabilizing force in her life, serving as an anchor in her dark hours. So, I believe that you gave birth, and life, to Gail, Erica. And she was truly blessed by your arrival and all the years you had together.*

*My hope is that she and Allie have found each other again in the great out there and are watching down on the two of us and smiling as you celebrate another birthday. Since you and I are getting older and they are not, maybe they are actually having the last laugh.*

*Love and aloha,*
*Mother Sheraton*

# Hubris

---

WHEN WILL AND I planned our two months at the beach near Gulf Shores, Alabama, one of my main objectives was to be able to reconnect with law school classmates who had been my friends for more than three decades. After I moved away from Alabama, I hadn't seen enough of them and my concern was that we were getting to an age when travel would be harder for us to manage. So part of our objective was to rent a really big house and have them come down for a mini-reunion at the beach.

Our law school class was divided into three sections, alphabetically. As my name at that time was Dayle Powell, I fell into section three, the O-Z section. In our first year, many of our classes were with our section members and the closest friendships tended to be with people whose last names were in the same part of the alphabet. So I planned a gathering including: Suzanne Paulson, Sandy Spivey, Rick Spivey, John Whitaker, Howard Rifkin, Lee Pittman, and Charlie Waldrep.

These were my closest friends for three brutal years of classes and all the years that came thereafter. We were godparents to each other's children, had been there through births, divorces, deaths, and funerals, and supported and encouraged each other through along the way. I love every one of them, and I know the feeling is mutual.

I dubbed the party the Big Chill, drawing on the famous movie that was all about school friends reuniting. I purchased copies of the movie and the CD as gifts for each of them. The invitation was formatted to look like the movie jacket but with each of our pictures on it instead of the actors'. I had t-shirts printed with the invitation on the back and *Res Judicata*, the thing speaks for itself, on the front. The classmates were invited to the beach to spend some time with a few good friends.

In the movie, the reason that the friends get together is that one of their own, Kevin Costner, who is actually never seen on camera, has committed suicide and they gather in their hometown for his funeral. One of the lines from the movie, spoken by Kevin Kline's character Harold, at Alex's funeral, was: *"Not all of us have been able to see each other much these last years. But neither time nor distance could break the bonds that we feel."* That was my sentiment entirely. The movie's weekend together resurrects vivid memories, lost hopes and dreams, as well as new ones and a fantastic assortment of the music of my generation is played throughout. The friends put their lives into perspective and reconnect in a powerful way. I envisioned us cooking together, telling stories, sharing hopes and dreams, challenging each other, and just hanging out for our Big Chill reunion.

Had I left it at that it would have been enough. But I just had to push it too far. Calling it the Big Chill Reunion would have evoked the right tone, spirit and good times that the movie managed to capture. My classmates are very smart people. They would have gotten what I was trying to create.

But hubris got the better of me.

I had to call it the Big Chill ... *without the dead body.*

At the time I wrote that, what I meant was that we shouldn't wait around for one of us to die before we all got together. Life is short. Life is passing. Life is unpredictable. Let's have fun now, while we are all still able to do it. Let's not wait around for someone's dead body to jolt us into action.

Did my hubris tempt fate? I don't really believe that. My logical, rational mind tells me that an irreverent, insensitive, arrogant remark doesn't cause the death of anyone. I didn't conjure up a dead body, Allie's, by being such a jerk. I didn't kill her. It is just that some might say I had it coming. All I can say is that it was less than a month after I wrote that provocative invitation that Allie died. Proverbs says that pride goes before a fall.

We had our class reunion at Allie's Celebration of Life, when all these friends and more showed up in Marietta, Georgia on a chartered bus in the midst of an ice storm. It was not the reunion I planned. It was the reunion I needed.

I know that if I could take back anything, I would take back that remark.

# The Birth Story of Lucas Woodford

A MYTHICAL BIRTH story for Lucas, with whom Allie went to the Junior Prom at Seabury Hall. Now a successful Maui realtor, Lucas always bore a strong resemblance to a famous person.

Written July 26, 2013

*Dear Lucas,*

*Happy Birthday, you Leo, you!*
*Being born on July 26th, means that fire is your element. You have a passionate side that is appealing and draws in others. And, you are slightly dramatic, warm and loving. In fact, you have amazing star quality! (It's not me saying this; it's astrology.)*

*What I want to say is to explain to you how it happened that you embody all these qualities, Lucas. You see I know the secret story of your birth. And for your birthday today I want to share it with you for the first time.*

*Now what I am about to tell you may come as something of a surprise, but I'm sure if you sit quietly on a beach for a while and just let it simmer in the back of your mind you will see the truthfulness of this birth story. It may allow you to fully understand, finally, some of the parts of your personality that have previously baffled you, and us.*

*You see, Lucas, this is not your first time at bat. You've been here before. That little baby boy who was born to your mom and dad thirty-two years ago wasn't coming to the earth for the first time. In fact, on his last appearance he was someone who was well known and even idolized by many. He was a person who embodied many of the same star qualities as you currently do. He was passionate, dramatic, warm, loving, and drawn to and governed by the fire element. Can you guess?*

*Let me give you some hints.*

*Have you ever wanted to drive through the south and just hang out for a while in small hamlets in places like Mississippi?*

*Do you ever feel your hip twitching almost uncontrollably?*

*Do you start moving as soon as you hear the first note of music being played? And, do you move faster if that music happens to be rockabilly, that strange combination of rock and hillbilly?*

*Do you have a strong urge to let your hair grow longer and to darken it?*

*Are you totally seduced by the smell of a fried banana sandwich? You know, that magical combination of white bread, Sunbeam preferably, peanut butter, sliced bananas and crisp bacon, buttered with real butter on both sides and then pan fried in a skillet?*

*Well, when these events occur, and they may happen daily, you are having a past life experience. A little window has opened from this lifetime to an earlier one you experienced.*

*And in that earlier life, you started out in Mississippi, although you migrated to Memphis as a teenager. From there you found your way to fame and fortune in the 50s and 60s.*

*Have you figured it out yet?*

*Well, dear Lucas, you are the reincarnation of none other than the King himself!*

*Yes, that's right. Elvis Presley. And that is why you always want a hunk, a hunk of burning love. And, why you will have to watch what you eat and don't let doctors overprescribe medicine for you.*

*It happened like this. When Elvis performed his Aloha concert from Honolulu, many years ago, he vowed that someday he would return and live in Hawaii. But, unfortunately, he wasn't able to achieve that goal in that lifetime, as he was overcome by an extreme bout of constipation and died straining at the stool. But his spirit was just waiting its chance to enter a body that would totally embrace his utter coolness. And he found that opportunity when you were born.*

*Welcome back, King! Don't be cruel to a heart that's true.*

*Love and aloha,*
*Dayle*

# Humility

FAST FORWARD, TWO years. Still in limbo. We had sold the tiny golf condo. We were living in a beautiful rented villa in Kapalua. We were on the mend, but a long way from being whole.

Early one morning I was home alone and Will had already gone to our offices. I had just taken a shower and was getting dressed for work as well. I left the bathroom for just a few minutes to get a cup of coffee and returned to do my hair and makeup. When I stepped into the room my feet slipped on a puddle of water that had formed in my brief absence. I almost fell down, but managed to catch myself on the door and wall.

Water was oozing into the room from the toilet. It was coming out the bottom of the toilet. My immediate response was two-fold. I turned off the water valve behind the bowl and I threw my towel onto the floor to try to mop up the spill.

The next few hours were like being trapped in a really bad movie. It was a literal shit storm. My towel quickly became soaked. The water was rapidly flowing into the room and by now was easily an inch deep. It had soaked all the floor mats as well. I grabbed every towel in the bathroom to try to absorb it all but it was no use.

I was now standing barefooted in water that was covering my toes and it was not clear water. It was grey, murky, foul-smelling water. Now it was no longer just coming out of the toilet, it was also gurgling up from the shower drain as well and it was getting darker and more rancid by the moment.

I gathered every single towel we owned, probably twenty or so and threw every one of them onto the floor of the bathroom but it wasn't enough. I called Will at the office in desperation. "Please come home and help me out here. I don't know what else to do."

Will came home immediately and he thought that maybe getting a bucket and squeezing out the towel before reusing it would help take the water off the floor. But he poured the filthy water into the sink many times without realizing it was just coming right back into the system before he abandoned that idea.

I also called a plumber but a traffic accident that morning had closed the main highway in Lahaina and no plumbers were able to respond immediately to our crisis. Will and I continued our losing efforts to stop the surging cesspool that was overtaking the condo and both of us became soaked with the smelling wastewater.

We called the villa management office to see if they could help. We now had three guys running in and out of our bathroom. And finally, after about an hour of sopping towels, bailing water, and standing in murky, filthy water a plumber arrived to shut down the system.

By now, the villa was thoroughly soaked from all the tracking back and forth. We were shell shocked by the speed with which our villa went from a fabulous place to live to a hazardous waste area. Every towel we owned was ruined, as were our shoes, the carpets, and so much more. We hadn't had a moment to think about the potential health hazard of all this because we were so caught up in the immediate water hazards. But later that afternoon, when a hazardous waste worker showed up to read the bacterial counts and assess the damage, he told us we had a level three environmental hazard in our villa.

Level three sounds pretty serious, but having no experience with anything at all like this, I asked the obvious question, "is there a level four?" Level four is when they bring in the HAZMAT suits and oxygen tanks.

We were now being told that we had to leave. It wasn't safe for us to live there anymore. All our towels, our shoes and anything that touched the water would have to be disposed of as hazardous waste materials. Not only that but we needed to immediately seek medical attention and have Hepatitis A shots.

It was *déjà vu* all over again. Hadn't we already fled from the Alabama beach when BP arrived to clean up their tar ball mess? Hadn't we already fled from Colorado when the walls closed in on us as winter was coming? Hadn't we already fled the golf condo when the renovations invaded our little tiny space? Hadn't we already fled the coffee farm idea when that became a dead end street? Were we trapped in a perennial shit storm ever since Allie died, or was it just our inability to cope that made every situation seem like a shit storm?

Would it ever end?

And just when we thought it really couldn't get any worse for us emotionally, when we were totally wrung out, spent, finished, defeated, Will looked at his wrist and realized that the whole time he had been bailing water and wringing out towels he was wearing the little string bracelet he bought at the beach in Alabama to remind him of Allie. The same water that forced us to evacuate the villa now defiled that precious symbol of his tie to her.

We cut it off his wrist and walked away.

It, too, was disposed of as hazardous waste.

# The Birth Story of Danielle Allaire

A MYTHICAL BIRTH story for Allie's high school classmate, with whom she drove the ninety miles, round trip to school and back, each day.

Written June 11, 2013

*Happy birthday Danielle!*

*Do you know what happened on June 11, 1982, in addition to you making your first ever appearance on the stage? It was also the day that the movie, ET, debuted. Coincidence? I think not!*

*You see, Danielle, it so happened that your mother, Jackie, was watching ET on the day you were born and she was deeply imprinted by what she saw. Like the rest of us, she instantly fell for the little guy Elliott brought home, with the large pointy fingers and great curiosity. She literally* couldn't take her eyes off the screen. It was as if she fell into a deep hypnotic trance and as he intoned, "ET phone home. ET phone home," she was more and more mesmerized by the whole scene.

Her daze was broken only by the screaming of the younger sister of Elliott when she opened the closet door in her bedroom to discover the presence of the little alien. That scream, pitched at the note of C sharp, above high C, was not only a memorable movie moment, but also literally the moment of your mother's awakening.

And just as she awoke, the nurse in the hospital nursery asked her if she had chosen a name for her baby girl and she said you would be named Danielle. Now Jackie and David had been discussing baby names for you for nine months. In fact they had gone through literally hundreds of them and nowhere on any of their lists or in any of their conversations was the name Danielle mentioned by either of them.

Danielle, as I'm sure you know, means judged by God. It is Hebrew in origin and comes from the male name Daniel, who was a great prophet and interpreter of dreams for the king. Even though your parents may have known this about the name, it still didn't make their long list of potential names for you.

So, where did it come from? You may well ask.

Well this is what happened.

The little girl who screamed that scream, pitched at the note of C sharp above high C, was none other than Drew Barrymore. Sixteen years and fifty days later, Drew Barrymore played the role of Danielle, also known as Cinderella, in the movie Ever After. As you know, Danielle was kind and loving and giving, in sharp contrast to her stepsisters and her wicked stepmother, played by Angelica Houston.

Physicists believe that certain high-pitched notes can literally reshape the time dimension of the universe if hit solidly enough and sustained long enough. It is as if the high, shrill note causes a kind of time warp. This phenomenon is referred to in the scientific literature as the C Sharp Dimension.

*Well, as Jackie watched ET while she recovered from your birth, and Drew screamed her famous, shrill scream, that is just what happened. Your mother looked into the future sixteen years and fifty days and saw that little girl actor developed into the lovely and charming Cinderella, known as Danielle. And your fate was sealed.*

*You became Danielle Allaire, lovely, charming, kind and giving. You owe it all to Drew Barrymore, and her fabulous vocal chords.*

*Happy birthday, Danielle! Here's to many, many more.*

# What is Not Helpful?

**W**HENEVER SOMEONE DIES, I think it brings out the best in human nature for the most part. People try to be thoughtful and kind. They go out of their way to say and do the right things. They are typically at a loss to know what to say or do, but they make an effort anyway, just because they feel they should at least try. We were shown so many kindnesses in the wake of Allie's death.

Like the doctor from Boston Medical Center who had been one of her attending physicians who called me an hour or so after she died to see if there was anything she could do to help me. She was the one I could tell to simply take out all the tubes and equipment and leave her alone in a darkened room to be at peace. This kindness allowed me to believe that Allie's soul could then quietly leave her body and make its journey without being hurt any more.

Like our friend and client, Ray Skelton, hopping on a plane from Maui to Marietta and being the very first person we saw when we got to the Strand Theatre on the morning of her Celebration of Life. We were carefully stepping onto and over black ice on the sidewalk, trying not to fall, and looked up and there he was, slipping and sliding, too. Seeing his face was both a shock and a comfort. We didn't even know he knew. But, being a loyal kind of guy, Ray's first response was just to be there.

Like my nephew and niece, Stephan and Donna, who not only took care of Guinness while we were in Marietta but who also made the gift bags for all the folks who came. Donna was madly trying to find bottles of bubbles, and tubes of glitter, and lots and lots of sidewalk chalk, and ribbons, and silver bags when every store was closed due to the weather. Their entire family showed up in wonderful costumes even though explaining to their kids that their cousin had died and now they needed to put on their Halloween costumes to go to her service must have been an interesting dinner conversation for them.

Like Allie's high school friend, Melissa, who asked permission to go see her at the morgue and to say the Kaddish prayers over her body. We weren't even Jewish, but what could it hurt? And Melissa also learning to play the violin in two weeks so that she could be part of the performance.

Like Betty Sakamoto shipping two thousand orchids from Maui to Marietta for the audience to be able to toss them onto the stage at the end of the Celebration, in the way that Hawai'ians place leis on the water when someone dies. Those orchids couldn't be delivered to the theater because of the ice storm but we were able to go to the warehouse and pick them up anyway. It was the perfect ending to a perfect celebration.

Like Doug Carney, not only working to produce the Celebration but also paying for a colleague to come do the live webcast so that our friends who couldn't be there could watch it, too.

Like Kareem Khubchandani, who managed to both direct and emcee the performance, doing so many costume changes in his role it was absolutely dizzying.

Like my law school classmates who chartered a bus from Birmingham to Marietta and put on makeup and costumes to show their support.

Like my sisters Carolyn and Ann who showed up at the beach house just to cook and clean for us for a few days while we were distraught.

Like our friends from the Sheraton Maui who dedicated the sunset ceremony in her memory and who filmed the cliff diver jumping from Black Rock into the ocean and sent it to us to become part of the Celebration of her life.

Like our family doctor, Norman Estin, who flew from Maui to Marietta to be there with us and for us. This was taking the concept of making a house call beyond all expectations.

And like so many hundreds of others who in so many ways showed their incredible love and support for us in our weakest moments, in our most vulnerable days, in our despair. They made it possible to bear it.

BUT, what was not helpful were the people who just were clueless about the impact of their words and deeds.

Like the person who said to me that God does not give us more than we can bear. I know she meant to be kind. I know she was just repeating something that she had heard in church and earnestly believed to be true. But, did she even consider the impact of those words on a mother whose child is dead? It made me think that if only I hadn't been such a strong-willed, hard working person maybe God would have let Allie live. It made me feel that I had somehow caused her death by being too uppity. If only I had been less able to bear the loss maybe she'd still be alive taking care of her weak mother.

Like the doctor who was grilling steaks next to Will months later and who was the head of cardiology at a big university hospital on the West Coast. His comment was that Allie died because she got sick on New Year's Eve when all the best doctors would have been on leave. And that she wouldn't have died if he had been there because he could have put her heart on a machine that would have kept it pumping until they defeated the virus. What was he thinking?

Like her employer who left her voice on the office answering system so that when we called the main number to ask about any possible life insurance benefits she may have had, it was Allie's voice we heard telling us the office was currently closed but please leave a message and she would return our call in the morning. Oh God. That was brutal.

Like my childhood friend who told me just to pray to Jesus, turn it all over to Jesus and he would bear it for me. I'm sorry, but where was the big guy when she was dying? How about a little miracle of recovery or raising from the dead if Jesus really wanted to be helpful? After she died no amount of platitudes would make a damn bit of difference.

Like the people who told me that I would never get over this. That we never recover from the death of a child. That we aren't supposed to bury our children. They are supposed to do that for us.

Like the friends who right after her death when I tried to tell them that we weren't victims and didn't see Allie's death as a tragedy, patted my hands and told me I was just in shock and would feel differently when some time had passed.

And like Facebook, who keeps sending me email reminders that Allison Powell is tracking things on the Internet or is friends with someone I may want to befriend.

# The Birth Story of Andrew Middleton

---

A MYTHICAL BIRTH story for Allie's high school classmate and fellow actor, who is now a neurosurgeon.

Written October 28, 2013

*Happy Birthday, Drew!*

*Or should I call you Dr. Middleton? After all, you have earned it. It has taken you a number of years and so much hard work to be entitled to be addressed with that honorific. Congratulations. Well done, you.*

*And now that you have achieved this high pinnacle of success, let me remind you where it all started, a little over thirty years ago today....*

*Your mother, Kathy, had come to Maui as a sun-loving, bikini-clad surfer girl, who could hardly be bothered to dry off as the next set of waves was always just ahead. Now Kathy was quite a package and many men* tried to make her their own *Wahine*, but she was having no part of it. She would grab her board and paddle beyond the break and wait for that perfect wave to begin to form before catching it and riding it all way back to the shore.

Drew, I know you have always believed that Eulie was your father, and it is true that he raised you as his own. So you were right to consider him a father figure. But if you want to meet your real father, then you have to get wet. Pick up a surfboard and head out beyond the surf break near Haiku, not far from Baldwin Beach. Be patient as it may take a while just hanging around as your mother did many years ago. In fact it may take several trips.

What you will be doing is signaling to the ones who are watching that you come in peace and you mean them no harm. When you have been around the area long enough and are trusted enough then you will likely find yourself, as your young mother did, encircled by a friendly pod of dolphins.

Yes, dolphins.

You see dolphins are the children of the sea, Drew. And on that beautiful afternoon some thirty years ago they were delighted to see Kathy again, playing and frolicking in the waves as she had so often before. And one particular dolphin, who was the alpha male of the pod, was named Andrew. He was gorgeous in that spinner dolphin kind of way, with a permanent smile on his face that seemed to suggest he knew something we don't know.

And, as a matter of fact he did. He knew that there is an attraction between alpha male dolphins and bikini clad women that can only be explained as animal magnetism. And when he smiled that spinner dolphin smile, your mother was smitten. He was the alpha to her omega, the yang to her yin. And he spun and he spun until she was mesmerized and she swam after him into a little protected cove where you were conceived.

You loved the period of your gestation, as it was not unlike swimming in the ocean for a long, long time. You were born ten months later (yes ten, *not nine. It takes longer to birth a dolphin-man). Knowing your biological origin, Kathy gave you a water birth, which made your entry into the world feel more natural. To your mother's great surprise, and no doubt the disappointment of your real father, you looked completely human, with no trace of your father's ancestry visible to the casual observer.*

*But your playful personality caused many to refer to you, even at an early age as the Ambassador of Aloha, a title your father Andrew had also enjoyed.*

*You had an early craving for squid and shrimp by the bucketful, which your mother gladly met. And you often spun in circles until you got so dizzy you would fall down. Other than these two little quirks, your childhood seemed quite human.*

*And so you grew into a dolphin-man, a doctor at that, who walks among us, like any other. And, of course, you ended up in Miami, the natural gathering place for dolphin-men.*

*And on certain full moon nights, you may find yourself seduced by the lulling sound of ocean waves, calling you home. Tides may come and go and you will discover yourself rocking slowly to their rhythm, being drawn back to the sea from which you sprang. Enjoy the journey, Drew, but be careful. There are sharks in the waters.*

# Grief

N MY PROFESSIONAL work I often start a meeting by having the participants introduce themselves with brief biographical statements, just a few sentences. Shortly after Allie's death, one woman began her introduction by saying she was a widow. At a break in the meeting, I expressed condolences and asked her when her husband had died. *"Ten years ago,* she said, with tears in her eyes, *"and every day I still grieve."*

With only a few sentences to introduce herself to a professional working group, she felt that her identity as a widow was the most important thing to tell the group. Although a decade had passed she had remained in a state of grief.

Folks used to say Alabama was a bad state to be in, but grief is worse by far.

Isn't it remarkable that in areas of Russia, Czechoslovakia, Greece, Italy, Mexico, Portugal and Spain, widows may wear mourning clothes for the rest of their lives? These customs are a relic of times when unattached women presented a threat to male dominance. What more effective way can there be of taking away women's power than relegating them to a life sentence of "widow's weeds?"

Grief is not a viable state for anyone's permanent address. While it is inevitable to go there from time to time, dwelling there is in no one's best interest. Moving away from grief into higher states of consciousness is one of the healthiest choices we can make. It does the dear departed ones no good for their survivors to dwell in grief for any extended period.

Jean Young, the wife of former Mayor Andrew Young of Atlanta, once told me that she and Andy had an agreement. Whichever one of them died first, the other would not let the bed get cold. She said it with a laugh, but that's a healthy way to move beyond grief and celebrate the love of a first marriage. The choice to love again and even remarry bears silent testimony to the enjoyment of marriage itself. After Jean's death, Andy later remarried.

Dr. David Hawkins, in his seminal book, "Power vs. Force, the Hidden Determinants of Human Behavior," ranks grief as one of the lowest levels of human consciousness, outranking only apathy, guilt, and shame. In a state of grief, one's life view is tragic and the principle emotion is regret. In grief, the feelings of powerlessness are almost overwhelming. A kind of despondency sets in and energy is drained from those around the person who is grieving.

So how does one move beyond grief? For some it may be incrementally, for others the shift may be exponential. Hawkins' research revealed that higher levels of consciousness above grief include fear, anger, pride and courage, among others. Some of these more elevated levels of consciousness can be the subject of our focused efforts and energies; others perhaps require the support of therapists, fellow survivors, or family.

At the Maui Transitions Center, we have seen so many cases where long suppressed feelings of grief can sabotage progress years later and can arise in almost unrecognizable ways.

For example, one of our clients was offered eight million dollars to stay on as a consultant when his company was sold. The new owner wanted to bring in his own CEO, but thought that person would benefit from our client's advice from the years he had served as the start-up CEO. The client was so angry about being rebuffed for the CEO position he was ready to walk away leaving eight million dollars on the table.

When he came to Transitions, we worked very hard with him for a week to help him remember and understand what led him to this critical point in his journey. And, after a number of homework assignments that included some good grief rituals he finally got clear about what was behind his seemingly irrational anger.

In high school this client had run for student body president and had lost the election. He was hurt. He was embarrassed. He was angry. But instead of processing his feelings at the time they occurred, he simply stuffed them for about forty years. They didn't go away. They were merely lurking in his subconscious like smoldering embers in a fire bed, awaiting the right conditions to burst into flames.

The client realized that when the new owner didn't want him to stay on in the CEO position it re-stimulated his high school feelings of rejection and he reacted in a childish, immature way initially. In Transitions he worked to truly grieve his loss of the student body election, including finally expressing all the anger he had tried to keep pent up for so long.

We literally had him beat a tree stump with a plastic baseball bat while yelling his anger at the top of his lungs. Once the anger was spent, he could re-evaluate the generous offer with more rational thought.

In another case, a woman who was so angry about the circumstances of the death of her son remained trapped in grief for at least five years after its occurrence. The death was sudden, accidental, and left behind a newborn child and young widow. The mother was holding onto anger so tightly, even after two years, that when speaking about the loss one could almost hear her teeth grinding as she spat out the words. Dwelling in anger, according to Dr. Hawkins', leaves us with a life view that is antagonistic and a primary emotion of hate. It is only a slightly elevated level of consciousness above grief.

One of the tools we use with clients in Transition would also be useful for someone who is struggling with grief. It is simple and could be used by anyone, anywhere. We first have them write a letter to the person who died. In the letter they can pour out anger, remorse, ask questions, give forgiveness, or just write any feelings or concerns that come to mind for them.

The next step involves them using their non-dominant hand to write a response from the dearly departed. So, if a wife, who is right handed, writes a letter to her husband who died, after that letter is complete, she then writes a reply from her husband using her left hand.

This process accesses both right and left-brain functions and often allows the client to get in touch with deeply held emotions that may not have been previously expressed. To make the experience more meaningful for the clients, we usually have them read their first letter out loud. Then, depending on the gender of the person who died, a staff member of the same gender reads the response. So, using this example, a male would read aloud the letter from her husband. This process drives home the message in a much more meaningful way and helps resolve tough issues for many of our clients.

For me, after Allie's death, on some days the grief felt overwhelming. Life was simply too hard. Getting out of bed seemed pointless. Yet sleep was impossible in the first months without Ambien. But I found that if I would just take the first step, just be willing to risk that the day might turn out okay, and then other things would seem to support my least effort to help myself. If I felt sad, I cried. But I tried to limit my crying to jags, not days, not weeks, not months.

Cry. Feel it. Move on.

Mourn. Express it. Move on.

Wallow. Help someone else. Move on.

When we find ourselves in a state of grief, we simply have to change our address and move on.

Whether we use anger, or desire, or pride, or courage, or even some combination of these higher states of consciousness, it is critical to our survival and our happiness to elevate ourselves above a grief level of consciousness. It is only by rising above it that we can reclaim our power in our lives. According to Dr. Hawkins, after we have done the work to rise above grief consciousness, we can aspire to find acceptance, joy and peace again.

We literally changed our address and moved on after Allie died. The harder work was in changing our consciousness and moving on to reclaiming joy and peace again in our lives. That is a work still in progress.

One day I happened on a banner with a quote attributed to Buddha that really spoke to the work I've been trying to do since Allie died. It hangs on my office wall.

*"A happy person is not a*
*person in a certain set of*
*circumstances, but rather,*
*a person with a certain*
*set of attitudes." (Buddha)*

# We Grieve Differently

SOME PEOPLE CALL me an expert in the application of Myers-Briggs typology. I've worked with this personality assessment tool for two decades with literally thousands of clients, so I'm supposed to know a few things about it. I wouldn't say I'm an expert, rather a student of the human condition and interested to learn more.

I know that Will and I are temperamentally opposite. That's part of the attraction, my yin to his yang. I'm an intuitive feeler and he is an intuitive thinker. I need to get in touch with my feelings to know what is true for me and what decision to make about an issue. He needs to get clear about his thinking and have a chain of logic to follow that makes sense to his way of thinking. I decide things based on my gut. He decides based on his head.

He wanted an autopsy because it was logical to want to know exactly what killed Allie and how she died. I felt that was wrong. A waste of money. A cruel thing to put her body and my psyche through. But I agreed. My types are peacemakers, looking for ways to harmonize decisions. It seemed easier for me just to suck it up and concede the point than put us all through even more stress and grief. He's from Mars. I'm from Venus.

Sometimes, when things are broken, I just need to process my feelings about it. That may mean crying a lot. Sometimes it even requires throwing myself a pity party, filling the bathtub with bubble bath and staying in it until my skin is shriveled and my tear ducts are depleted. Sometimes it means scream therapy, putting a pillow in my face to blunt the noise, and screaming at the top of my lungs until my throat hurts just so that I'm not suppressing my emotions. And sometimes, when it is really rough, it may mean wearing gloves and taking a plastic baseball bat to a stump and beating it so hard that the bat may actually break, all the while yelling out my feelings. I've not only done all these processes myself, I also advise clients to use them to release pent up anger or grief. I need to talk about feelings, to externalize them, to extravert them. I'm not one for pent up feelings.

As an introvert, Will is a master of pent up feelings. Introverts tend to internalize their feelings, processing them quietly, analyzing them, and thinking them through before expressing them. We tend to misunderstand introverts because they can come across as cold and unfeeling. The truth is that their feelings are just as strong as extraverts' feelings. We just don't hear as much about them, while extraverts tend to wear theirs on their shirtsleeves.

My feelings can be pretty scary stuff to my introverted husband. It hurts him to see me grieve. He wants to help. He wants to fix things. I don't need things to be fixed, especially when they can't be fixed. I just want him to let me vent my feelings about how broken they are. He can only take so much of that before he has to run away from me. I can only take so much of his running away from me before I think the thing that is really broken is us.

He has a delayed reaction response to bad things. I have a hair trigger response. My feelings erupt like a volcano. His simmer below the surface like magma, boiling hot and potentially explosive. We grieve differently. But that doesn't mean we grieve less deeply. It took me a long time to understand that simple truth.

This journey has brought out the best of the worst and us. We have had some of the bitterest arguments as well as some of the tenderest expressions of kindness and understanding. I'm sure we each have thought at times that our relationship would not survive the storm.

One thing we share is our shadow. It is the part of the personality that is the least mature. It is the part of us that feels out of control. It is also the part we lead with when we are under too much stress. For both of us that part of our undeveloped personality is sensing, taking things in through our senses by seeing, touching, smelling, tasting. It can also mean becoming obsessed with insignificant data that really doesn't matter.

For folks like us, with sensing as our inferior function, stress can be endured if there is sufficient ice cream, or wine, or popcorn, or any other pleasurable sensation that we indulge. I have gained forty pounds since Allie died. Will has gained about the same amount. It's not like we want to eat an entire pint of rum raisin, it is more like eating the whole pint will allow us to endure the thing that triggers the eating binge to start with. It distracts us from the real problem.

We will know we are finally healing when we have gotten back to healthy weights and lifestyles. I'd say Will is doing a better job of that right now. I still have a ways to go.

# The Birth Story
# of Polly Morton

A MYTHICAL BIRTH story for Allie's college friend and San Francisco neighbor, Polly.

Written October 2, 2012

*Happy birthday, Polly!*

*I am sure you have spent many days and nights wondering how your wonderful parents ever came up with your name. Looking at the face of a newborn baby and deciding by what name it will be known for the rest of its life is a daunting task for anyone, and your parents were no exception. Believe me, they struggled for nine full months before deciding. Here's how it went.*

*Your dad originally wanted to call you Polly Wog. That is because he loved to fish and he often watched tadpoles swimming around the shorelines as he cast his bait into the streams and lakes. Those little tadpoles were* so cute, and so carefree. He began to imagine that you were like them, just a little tadpole swimming around in your mother's belly, growing and growing. He came home one day with his catch and announced to your mother that he wanted to name you Polly Wog when you were born. Well, your mother was having no part of that! She yelled at him that everyone knows that pollywogs grow up to be frogs and no one was going to be calling her baby a frog! So that one got nipped in the bud.

Your mom thought you should be called Pollyanna, as she had just read the wonderful book about the orphan who managed to find things to be glad about in every situation, no matter how dreadful it was. Even when she wanted a doll for Christmas and got a crutch that she didn't even need, she was glad that she didn't need a crutch, instead of being bummed about not getting a doll. Your mom thought Pollyanna was a lovely, lyrical name and it just rolled off her tongue every time she said/sang it. But your dad said, come on! No child of his was going to be branded with a name that would make everyone think she was naïve.

Then your dad came up with the really lame-brained idea of calling you Polly Wolly Doodle All the Day! I think he must have been stationed in Louisiana during his military service and he and the guys had sat around drinking and singing that ditty late into the night so that it was etched permanently on his brain. When he suggested calling you that, your poor mother just broke into tears and ran out of the room. They made up and he agreed never to bring it up again, ever!

And your mom also wanted to call you Polly Pureheart. She had been spending a lot of time with her feet elevated watching cartoon reruns and she had seen Polly Pureheart being tied to the railroad tracks by evil villains then rescued just as the locomotive was bearing down on her frail body. Polly Pureheart was a great believer that all would turn out well in the end. Your mom admired her faith. But your father preferred a daughter who would more likely rescue herself than wait for some guy to show up.

And so, after months of heated debate, they settled on Polly. Just Polly. Wonderful Polly. And aren't we all glad they did?

# Belief Systems

RECENTLY I HAD to go to our local emergency room for some testing. It wasn't really an emergency, just some inexplicable abdominal pain that developed on a weekend night when no doctor's office could see me. So we drove to the other side of Maui to be seen in the ER. As I was checking in they were asking me the standard questions to be sure their records were up to date.

Name?

Date of Birth?

Address?

Insurance?

Next of Kin?

Religious Preference?

When they got to that one, I simply replied, "No, thank you."

The lady said, "the last time you were here you said you were Methodist."

"Well, that was a long time ago, in a galaxy far, far away."

I guess I actually started out in this life as a Methodist. My grandfather was a deacon in a Methodist church in Talladega, Alabama. As a child I had attended Vacation Bible School at a Methodist church in my hometown of Anniston, Alabama. I loved going to Vacation Bible School because there were such fun art projects and we got treats, like Kool-Aid and cookies, every day. But when the pastor came by to pray for the class and to see if any of us wanted to be saved, I kept my head down. I was into the pinecone wreaths, but not the surrendering all to Jesus part of Methodist beliefs. My husband, who comes from a small family, has three ordained Methodist ministers and two lay ministers in his close family circle. When we moved to Maui we attended the Lahaina United Methodist Church. I even served on the Pastor/Parish relations committee. So I have lots of ties to Methodist beliefs.

But at age eight, I was baptized as a Mormon. My sisters were also baptized. My parents were Mormons, more in word than in deed. I grew up in the Mormon Church, even played the organ for the services. It was mostly a good influence in my life. Taught me right from wrong. Kept me a virgin until I got married. Made me want to go to college. Those are all good things. But I just couldn't square the fact that Mormons didn't allow women to hold the priesthood, which was the power to act for God. If you were a female Mormon, you were mostly meant to marry a male Mormon and raise a big Mormon family. Having come from a big Mormon family, I couldn't see myself replicating my mother's role. It looked a lot like a trap to me. And I also couldn't understand how this perfect heavenly father could be such a racist. The Mormon Church I grew up in drew the line at letting black folks in. It seems that God had placed the mark of Cain on their race and they were being forever punished for the sins of their forefathers. Or some such nonsense, which in the racist South of my youth had a lot of appeal to a lot of folks, but somehow to me didn't seem credible. So when I went away to college, I also went away from the Mormon Church. I used to say I was a Mormon until I learned to read. But the truth of the matter is that I was an early reader. I can't honestly claim such insight.

Interestingly, God himself must have learned to read the handwriting on the wall some years later as Mormonism changed after I left the faith. Seems that they had a new revelation that God no longer cursed Black people. They could now be baptized and the men could even hold the priesthood. I can't imagine that either the Civil Rights Movement, or new legislation prohibiting racial discrimination would have influenced God in any way. Maybe he just decided that he had marked these people long enough and they should be allowed to join like the rest of his flock, and pay their full ten percent tithing, of course. For the life of me I couldn't understand any Black person wanting to be a member of a faith that for so many years thought they were less than worthy to belong. It just seemed like there was a Groucho Marx one liner in there somewhere. God still seems to be of the opinion that women are not worthy to act for him and Mormon women are still relegated to supportive roles. So, for most of my life I have been seen as a Jack-Mormon, which is how they view someone who fell away from the faith. I guess I would have wanted at least to be seen as a Jill.

Allie's father, Don Powell, was a lifelong Baptist. So when she and her older brother, Geoff were infants, we took them up to the front of the Baptist Church and dedicated their lives to God. Members of the congregation agreed to accept them into the community and support them on their spiritual journey. I was never a Baptist. They aren't allowed to dance. What would life be without dancing? Why in the world would God possibly disapprove of that joyous act?

So my kids weren't raised in a religious tradition, more of a spiritual one. One that included a belief in the existence of the soul, the divinity of every human being, the respect for people of all faiths, as well as for people with no faith, and a keen eye for hypocrisy. It felt worse to me to see a Jimmy Swaggert or a Jim Baker charlatan doing more harm to religion by not walking their talks than to see an atheist openly questioning its basic tenets. Jimmy Buffet sang that religion was in the hands of some crazy-assed people, and I had to say I agreed with that sentiment. Religion is a mess. Spirituality is not.

Allie struggled with these mixed messages her entire life. She had Black Mormon friends. She had Kabala-practicing Jewish friends. She had Methodist and Presbyterian ministers all around her. I left it up to my children to decide for themselves if they would join any religion, or none. She never opted for any one of them. But she did see many ties between religious worship services and performance art. She was more interested in viewing how theatrical influences played a role in our religious convictions. Would a pope be seen as less powerful without the robes and the red slippers? How does drama impact on our experience of any worship service? How do we mix costuming, props, wardrobe and sound effects to deliver a religious experience as profound as any other form of performance art?

In San Francisco she sometimes attended the church services at Glide in the Tenderloin district. She felt at home there. It spoke to her soul. The roof raising music of the choir. The theatrical antics of the minister. And the stand up and clap and tap your feet, join in the celebration spirit of the congregation were all elements that she connected with deeply, but not deeply enough to join.

When she died a psychic told me that Allie's soul was ready to move on because she had work to do beyond the physical realm. She drew a picture of Allie as a large, angelic creature that was holding the earth in her palms. She believed that Allie's death was freeing her from the limitations of this earthly plane so that she could fulfill her soul's purpose.

What do I believe?

I believe that she is still here with me. That she still is connected to me at a soul level. That she is a loving, divine presence in my life.

That she still cares about not only the people she knew when she was alive but also about all of us, every soul, living or dead. That she is connected to other souls as well. That she sends me messages of loving-kindness from time to time, as do others of my departed family members.

That she is happy. That she is exactly where she is supposed to be, doing what she is supposed to be doing.

That someday I will encounter her again, but not in this life.

That part of the reason she was so fearless was that she knew death was not the end of her journey. It was just the transition point for the next great adventure.

That I have to let her go, just like I had to let her go off to college, or off to Australia or Scotland. She needed the experience to grow into her full potential.

That I was just the bow. She was the arrow.

That it was my deepest privilege to have given birth to her in this life. That in the next life, she may give birth to me.

That as hard as I tried to be her teacher, she was mine, perhaps my greatest teacher.

That I have so much more to learn.

That it isn't my time to transition yet, but when it comes, she will be my soul's guide. I'm looking forward to seeing her again.

# Turning the Corner

HOW DOES ANYONE ever know when he or she is coming out of the long dark tunnel of grief? Is it when they can make it through the first day without tears? Is it when they can sleep through the night without nightmares or pills? Is it when the flashbacks stop? Is it when they can look at a picture of the one who died and feel joy for the time they had together, rather than longing or remorse for what was missed? Is it when they can smile or truly feel happy again after believing they never would?

For me, the awareness came in the midst of yet another disaster.

Our home in Colorado is in Estes Park, a lovely small town located at the entrance to the Rocky Mountain National Park, at an elevation of 7,522 feet above sea level. It is a classic western mountain town, with more elk than people, and we like it like that. It is quiet. People are real. And nature is spectacular.

We returned to Estes in the fall of 2013 to enjoy the change of seasons and to reconnect with some of those same law school friends who had been scheduled to come to Fort Morgan, Alabama for our Big Chill reunion almost three years earlier, but who had ended up in Marietta, Georgia, instead.

Will and I knew we were getting better. We were crying less, sleeping more. We were laughing for joy again, not just through tears. We were definitely on the mend. And so we thought we were up to having friends come and stay with us in our mountain home. They were there for five days of good times. Not quite like the old days, but not so far off either.

Every afternoon was marked by the usual late summer thunderstorms that boom through the mountains and good, cooling rains. We enjoyed the storms by the fireplace as we shared our memories, and our truths with each other. The rains didn't damper our spirits; rather they encased us in a quiet, comfortable space.

After five days our friends left but the rains continued. In fact, they became a deluge, a storm of epic proportions. Fifteen inches of rain fell in four days. Our mountain town became the epicenter for a flood that had not been equaled in a thousand years. The water that had started in the mountains above Estes Park swelled the two rivers in the town and overflowed their banks sweeping away bridges, roads, cars, houses, livestock, farms, and fortunately very few people.

The main street, Elkhorn Avenue, ran like a river itself with water moving so fast that it created current, jetties, and even an undertow. Town was virtually locked down. Buildings were closed and shuttered. Sand bags blocked the entrances to almost every door. No restaurants in town were open. No shops. In a town whose survival depends on tourist dollars, an eerie stillness fell upon the empty streets. All of Estes quickly became a no-go zone. Large concrete barriers were erected to block entry into town. National Guard troops blocked the main highways. We were being hemmed in on all sides, limited to a smaller and smaller area of existence.

We were cut off from the rest of the state, as the two major roads coming up to the mountain from the Front Range were simply gone for many miles. There was one road over the top but it was restricted to emergency vehicles and supplies. The only other road had one lane that could be used. Residents were told that if we went down the mountain we might not be allowed to come back up again. All tourists were told to leave so as not to be an additional drain on emergency supplies and resources.

Power went out, as did cell phone towers. Almost the whole town became a no flush zone as raw sewage was being dumped into the swollen rivers when the infrastructure was destroyed. There was no way to communicate with family and friends in the initial days after the flood. Panic buying caused our Safeway shelves to be emptied pretty quickly of bottled water, batteries, and firewood. Food supplies were low, too. The town sold out of gas leaving only diesel fuel at any of the pumps.

All around us houses were flooding and neighbors were stranded when bridges washed away. Many friends took the option to evacuate down the single lane road to get away. Some decided to shelter in place and wait it out. After all, this was not the first time Estes Park had flooded and they were mountain folk, strong, rugged.

Each day at 10:00 a.m., the residents who were able to leave their houses gathered at the Town Hall to listen to the latest emergency briefings by public officials. We heard about helicopter rescues of families stranded on the wrong side of destroyed bridges and roads. We were advised about emergency shelters, Red Cross food supplies, and areas to avoid due to damaged roads and dangerous gas mains that might explode.

Our home was watertight. Not a single drop had penetrated even our basement areas. We were high and dry while all around us people had mud in lower levels of their homes, or even running water coursing through their living areas. The initial damage was caused by floodwaters. As time went by, the growing fear was of falling trees or mudslides from areas that had burned in the previous year's fires.

Just across the street from our home, two large blue spruce trees had fallen into the river above our bridge. The Colorado blue spruce is a giant tree, capable of reaching heights of forty to fifty feet and more. The two fallen trees were easily that. If the floodwaters kept swirling long enough those trees had the potential to break loose and ram into the bridge that connected our neighborhood to the town. With the right conditions, they could still destroy our only outlet. That was the biggest potential threat to our safety that we could foresee.

With poor sanitation conditions there was also rising concern about health issues. Our little hospital didn't have the necessary neonatal oxygen equipment should a baby be born prematurely and with helicopters being used for evacuations; there was no guarantee that a baby could be taken to better hospitals down the mountain. The elderly population was also at increased risk of medical emergencies.

The daily news updates were not encouraging. We needed to make a decision to stay or go. We had a perfectly good home on Maui awaiting our return. There was no compelling reason to keep us in Estes Park since our home there was secure. Common sense would say that we should simply leave.

As I weighed all these factors, everything on the side of rational thought weighed heavily in favor of evacuating. But from deep within me came a stubborn resistance to that chain of logic.

We had run away from the Fort Morgan beach house when British Petroleum's arsenal of clean up equipment made it unbearable, we had fled from Colorado to avoid the cold darkness of our first winter without Allie, we had fled the tiny condo when renovations made recovery there impossible, we also fled the shit storm in the villa. I was sick and tired of feeling like a refugee. Running away hadn't solved any problems we faced. It was merely avoiding facing them. I felt on some level that leaving was an admission that we couldn't cope with life's problems; we weren't capable of managing our own affairs anymore.

And so it was that several days into the floods, when things were looking really bad in Estes Park, right after we had returned from yet another town briefing on the emergency response level, I asked Will to sit down with me to talk about our options. As much as I expected him to say we should evacuate, he and I were on the same page about what we should do. We both wanted to stay.

If we stayed we could at least help our friends whose homes were damaged or who didn't have the necessary supplies to bail out the water or be able to manage in a no flush zone. And so we spent the next week helping repair the home of one of our friends, and helping create a temporary port a potty from our camping supplies for another. We took food to friends whose road was so damaged they couldn't get to the grocery store. It wasn't much, but it wasn't running away.

And then, about a week after the flood we noticed fire and rescue trucks from Littleton, Colorado had come up the mountain on the single lane road and were across the street where the spruce trees had fallen. For three days those volunteers worked to take the limbs off the fallen trees and remove their trunks from the river. They wore wet suits and helmets and belayed themselves on ropes to safely excavate the biggest threat to our safety. When their work was finished we breathed a huge sigh of relief.

We thanked those brave men who volunteered to help us. As we walked back up the street to our home it was as if we were starting a new chapter, or maybe we were just ending a long, painful one. It was time to move on.

As bad as it was to be in an epic flood, we learned that we were stronger than we knew. Maybe the series of bad things that had happened to us over the previous two and a half years were also making us tough. We were bowed but not broken. Perhaps we had turned a corner, at long, long last.

# Lessons Learned the Hard Way

"*E*XPERIENCE KEEPS *a dear school, but fools will learn in* no other." Benjamin Franklin

February 2014

Three years have now passed since Allie died. Although I would have to say they have been the three hardest years of my life, good things, as well as bad, have come from them.

On the good side of the ledger, I have become more fully present, both with myself and with others. I live much more in the moment than either the past or the future. I am keenly aware of the kindnesses of others and try to be quick to express appreciation to them. And, I have become aware that I have a reservoir of strength that is much deeper than I knew.

On the negative side, it must be said that I still have trouble sleeping. I regularly awaken at 1:00am, the time when we received the first call from the Boston Medical Center telling us Allie had been found non-responsive and wanting to know the family's wishes, and I am wide awake until after 4:00am, the time when they called us back to say that she had just been pronounced dead. On some subconscious level, even in sleep, I am still traumatized by the shocking way in which she left us far too soon. Ambien gives me some respite from this cycle. But when I don't take it, the dance begins again. It leaves me with a Hobson's choice between sleeplessness and a reliance on Ambien, which I have been assured, is not harmful even when used long term. Ambien feels like a crutch to me. So I fluctuate between using the crutch for a while, then trying to walk without it, then finding I need to revert to the crutch again.

And, I have also gained forty pounds. This is my next challenge, losing the weight and taking better care of myself.

I have tried to learn from this experience, as difficult as it has been to be a student under such exquisitely painful tutelage. Some part of me believes that if I can just mine the lessons and use them to help others dealing with their own losses then maybe it can be said that some good came from the bad. This belief has caused me to read many books on bereavement, loss, recovery, spirituality, past lives, and trauma, and to explore the meaning of death with devout religious believers as well as psychics and mediums.

What it all comes down to for me are a few simple lessons learned the hard way, small nuggets that condense a lot of painful processing into something that someone else may find memorable or useful. For what it may be worth, here's what I've learned:

1. Talk about it. Don't clam up. When we talk about a traumatic experience, our brain stores the memory in its historical data banks. It makes it part of our past, not so much in our present. Talking about it not only allows us to realize that we have already survived it, but also to seek guidance, help, and understanding from others.

   I have come to the place where I can talk about the death of my only daughter without crying. Three years ago, I would not have believed that was possible.

2. Our feelings are legitimate, even the angry, ugly ones. Growing up in Alabama, we were taught never to speak ill of the dead. But beliefs like that may cause us to repress genuine anger about the circumstances of their death, or the way their life impacted ours that prevents our own recovery. For example, if someone died in a car accident but they were driving drunk, or speeding excessively, don't we have a right, indeed a need to say how angry we are that their own actions caused us such grief and despair?

   Stuffing the anger we feel about our loss can prevent us from remembering the joyous times as well.

3. The path to recovery is unique. There is no formula that will insure a good outcome. There is no magic pill, not even Ambien that guarantees we will heal. For some, working with a trained therapist or psychiatrist is the best path. For others, joining a support group, like Compassionate Friends, or a church group may provide solace faster. Some have a need to simply retreat from life for a while, to take a solo journey that allows them to go within to seek healing. Grief only takes as long as it takes. It is not a linear progression. There is no logical iteration. One day we may be doing just

fine and the next we sink into an abyss of sadness. There is no road map to recovery. And, giving up the need for direction, expectations, and a clear path may actually speed our healing process.

I do not know where this journey will lead me, nor do I have a sense of how to get there. All I know is that today I will do what I can to heal.

4.  I am not in control. It is not up to me. For most of my life I have lived with the illusion of control. I believed that if I obeyed the speed limit and drove carefully then I would not have a traffic accident. I thought if I followed the rules, obeyed the law, then my life would be better for it. But one only has to watch the evening news to realize that life is full of chaos. The universe is not an orderly place that responds perfectly to our beliefs and practices. As parents we do everything we can to protect our children and keep them safe. For years I preached the religion of using sunscreen, not smoking, not doing drugs, not drinking and driving, and practicing safe sex. Then my daughter died from the flu. I was powerless to prevent it.

    All my admonitions, my little axioms meant nothing to this virus.

5.  Allie's death impacted each of us differently. For me, it was the loss of my only daughter, and with it, the loss of certain expectations: that someday I would see her married, that she would bear my grandchildren, that she would finish her graduate education, even that she might take care of me in my old age. I lost my closest biological match, the person I believed understood me in ways that no one else could.

But since her death, I have learned that her brothers lost their closest confidante. They lost the person who shared their history and knew their story from the same vantage point. Sometimes she was the one with whom they were the most competitive, but she was also the one who could help them make sense of the whole dating scene and understand what women really want from men.

Will lost his only daughter, too, the little girl on whom he could dote, and who looked to him for guidance and advice. He lost the one who could go toe to toe with him in any debate or discussion of thorny issues. She may not have been his biological daughter, but he had loved her no differently than if she were.

And her friends and lovers suffered a loss that was difficult and painful to them in unique ways as well. Maybe she was the one who connected with their soul, or got their sense of humor, or saw them for who they truly were meant to be. Maybe she was the first or only one to love them unconditionally.

My pain may not be the same as their pain, but pain is still pain.

6. As bad as this has been, some families have it worse. This is perhaps the hardest lesson I have learned and maybe offered the greatest insight to me. When Allie died, so suddenly and I felt completely lost and totally bereft, I believed that no pain could be greater or depth of despair deeper than where I was. With hindsight and a lot of work, I have come to see that it could have been worse. Most people would agree that the death of a child is the worst loss. But even in this category of deaths, there are degrees of difficulty that impact our ability to recover. Allie was healthy and happy

for her entire life. It was only in the space of a very few hours that she could even be said to be ill.

Some families face not only the death of a beloved son or daughter, but special circumstances that add to their suffering. If she had died by fire, plane crash, drowning, poisoning, or other painful means would not our recovery process be more difficult? What if we felt some degree of complicity or responsibility for her death? Worse yet, if she had been the victim of a crime or murdered, we might have had to deal with the complications brought on by a criminal justice process that could take years to resolve, or might never be resolved if the criminal were not even caught. And, perhaps the greatest despair would come from the death of a child by suicide. Could we ever get to a place where we didn't blame ourselves for the loss?

My belief is that the death of a child by even the worst-case scenario is something from which we can ultimately recover. But my heart goes out to families dealing with such losses and my mind tells me that they need a special kind of understanding and support to cope. If I could offer them any advice, it would be to invoke the power of forgiveness to help us heal. Forgiving anyone who contributed in any way to the death of their beloved son or daughter and, most importantly, forgiving themselves as well, may be the best course of action they can take.

Forgiveness sets *us* free.

7. Don't allow yourself to dwell on your loss all the time. In the weeks and months immediately following the death of a loved one, this is almost impossible to achieve. But with the passage of time, it becomes easier to focus our attention on other things and other people. I tried to limit my crying

jags as an initial step. It is exhausting to cry all day long and it is scary to watch.

I learned that it was okay to cry in the shower because tears look just like water and no one would notice. I learned that it was never okay to cry while driving. With some effort I learned to focus enough to read again, work a crossword puzzle, or answer an email.

Although it initially irritated me when other people wanted to tell me about the deaths of their family members, or even their pets (!), I learned that if I listened I might actually gain some insight. I also learned to be able to comfort those who started on this journey after I did. Listening is the greatest gift we can give them. I find that I now ask, *"How are you doing, really doing?"* and want to hear the answer.

8.  It is important to memorialize our loss in some way. I believe strongly in the power of rites and rituals to help us make sense of life and to heal. Whether the memorial takes the form of a carved granite headstone, a single cross along a highway, a newly planted tree, a scholarship fund, or even a bronzed figure in a park, creating some tangible reminder of the person we have lost is one way of showing our love and our grief. It may also give us a kind of closure.

    In the Jewish tradition, one year after the death, the permanent marker is placed on the gravesite. In the Buddhist faith, one year later a paper lantern may be released on the water to commemorate those whose souls have sailed to a distant shore. Because of the generous support of so many friends and family, we were able to dedicate a courtyard in Allie's memory at the performing arts center on her high school campus. We also created a starving artists endowment in her memory at the Filament Theatre in Chicago. Now, with the award of Allie's Gift each year we feel a degree of satisfaction that the things that she really cared about live on.

But this type of closure doesn't require money. It merely requires sensitivity to the things that made our loved one the unique person they were. It can be achieved by anything as simple as quiet meditation in their memory, or writing a poem, or creating a painting. Or merely gathering a few friends and family together in their memory on an anniversary date or birth date. Or even offering a toast to their memory at a special meal.

There is no one right way to do this. We must each find our way.

9. Focus on what remains. This one takes some real effort. It is so easy to take stock of all that is lost and how our lives are negatively impacted by death. The awareness of what is missing comes unbidden to our minds in our first waking thoughts. But focusing on what remains may be the thing that makes it possible for us to get out of bed and face the day ahead.

This is really, really important when we have other children who still need us as parents. As well it matters a great deal to our spouses or life partners, who are also suffering and maybe can't heal by themselves. Even if we are the last survivor of a family line, what remains is *us*, the one who carries the family's history and can tell the story of those who went before.

It may be that it will be necessary to make lists of what remains in order to shift obsessive thoughts initially. If all we did was write the names of our living children on a note pad by our bed each night that might be enough to remind us that our work isn't done.

For me, telling this story, finishing it and getting it published was a big task that remained. It was a thing that kept me from just giving up when it all felt so bad. I felt that I owed it to Allie to share our story with a larger audience for whatever healing message it might bring.

And,

10. Thoughts of your own death will subside with the passage of time. In all of my reading after Allie died, I learned how often otherwise sane, healthy people contemplate suicide following the death of a loved one. This was both surprising and comforting to me. When I thought that my life ended when hers did and that I had nothing left to live for, the realization that these thoughts are common for survivors helped me hold on until they subsided.

Sometimes I thought that I would surely get a dreaded disease and die from that. After all, the death of a child is considered to be a "catastrophic stressor" by the Diagnostic and Statistical Manual of Mental Disorders. Would not this much anxiety, sleeplessness, grief and feelings of hopelessness surely culminate in cancer, or a heart condition, or something else deadly? Statistically speaking, it would.

And when I went for weeks and months without any joy, or laughter, the thought of even accelerating my own death did occur to me. But I had been through the suicide of a dear friend and knew the devastation that follows such a death. For me, the general idea never progressed to the point of making a plan or having a dress rehearsal. It just loomed somewhere off in the distance as an exit strategy.

If you do have such thoughts and you do begin to formulate such a plan, please, please get help immediately. Just vocalizing the degree of your pain will begin to alleviate it. You can call a crisis hotline, talk with a trusted friend, or family member, or see your doctor, therapist, or spiritual advisor.

There is no shame in asking for help when we need it. And that simple ask can be the beginning of our road to recovery.

# A Last Word From Allie

SINCE ALLIE HAD the first word in this book, it seems only fitting that she should also have the last.

In 1993 Will and I took Matt and Allie (Geoff was in summer camp) on a family vacation to Yellowstone National Park. Yellowstone is a spectacularly beautiful place, rich with wild life and lush with old growth trees. It is also a place of some significance to our family as Will's father, S. Seward Spencer, known to all as Bud, had worked at the Park for seven years during his early adulthood in the 1930s. Bud had been the Assistant General Manager of the bright yellow Yellowstone Lake Hotel. So our trip was a bit nostalgic and Bud seemed to be right there with us every step of the way.

Five years before our visit a massive fire had struck Yellowstone. The summer of 1988 was called the Summer of the Fires, as the largest wildfire in the recorded history of the Park burned for several months. In part, the conflagration was due to a change in fire management strategies. Whereas previously, the approach had been to suppress any wildfire as soon as possible, forest management theory had begun to acknowledge the benefit of periodic controlled fires to reduce the likelihood of major devastation when dry leaves and brush or fallen trees were allowed to accumulate over time.

1988 was an especially dry summer. When Park rangers began to set small, so-called controlled fires, they took off like rockets and leapt across roads leaving large blackened swaths in their paths. Over the summer of 1988, almost 800,000 acres of Parkland was burned, more than a third of the Park's total area.

Tens of millions of trees were killed.

Trees have always been my sanctuary. From my earliest childhood, when we were too poor to afford many toys, my sister Carolyn and I would climb into the Sycamore tree in our front yard and imagine that we were going on train trips, or sailing away to distant lands. I'm happy whenever I can be around trees and love the smell of being in a forest. Will and I have spent many a great holiday camping or hiking through forested wildernesses.

Naturally, we wanted to share Yellowstone with our children, both to connect them with Bud more deeply, and for its sheer beauty. So we found our way to Yellowstone five years after the devastating fires had struck. I was not emotionally prepared for what we would see.

My first impressions of the Park were of both its beauty and its great sadness. And I was overwhelmed by the destruction. There were times when all I could see were burned trees. It was like a massive black graveyard, haunted by ghostly stumps. I thought I could still smell the scorched earth although it had been years since the last whispers of smoke had dissipated.

As we drove on my spirits slumped. I was awash in feelings of gloom and doom. I'm sure my comments and deep sighs were depressing to the whole family. But Allie made me look again. From her post in the back seat of our rented car she made me look really closely at the ground. And there I could see little tiny green shoots poking through the charred remains. Literally, right in front of my eyes thousands of new trees had already begun to grow.

After our day's drive, we all wrote letters to Bud that we mailed to him and he later returned to us for our family photo album. This is what Allie said to her Grandfather at age eleven.

*"Yellowstone was a beautiful peace (sic?) of nature reserved and preserved for animals to live in and for people to see. I enjoyed it very much.*
*I also saw the burned trees.*
*I didn't think it was an end to have them all dead.*
*I thought it was a chance for rebirth!*
*Love, Allison"*

And, with the passage of the last three years, that is how I've come to see things, too.

# Suggested Reading

T HE BOOKS LISTED below were helpful to me in my journey. While I don't think it is possible to simply read our way out of grief, the company of a good author can certainly help along the way.

1. Alexander, Eben, M.D., **Proof of Heaven, A Neurosurgeon's Journey into the Afterlife**, Simon & Schuster Paperbacks, New York 2012.
2. Bernstein, Judith R., Ph.D., **When the Bough Breaks, Forever after the Death of a Son or Daughter**, Andrews McMeel Publishing, Kansas City, Missouri1998.
3. Didion, Joan, **The Year of Magical Thinking**, Vintage Books, New York, 2005.
4. Frankl, Viktor E., **Man's Search for Meaning**, Beacon Press, Boston, 2006.

5. Kubler-Ross, Elisabeth and Kessler, David, **On Grief and Grieving,** Scribner, New York, 2005.

6. Kushner, Harold S., **When Bad Things Happen to Good People**, Anchor Books, New York, 1981.

7. Mitchell, Byron Kathleen, **Loving What Is**, Harmony Books, New York, 2002.

8. Rinpoche, Sogyal, **The Tibetan Book of Living and Dying**, Harper San Francisco, 1993.

9. Rosof, Barbara D., **The Worst Loss**, Henry Holt and Company, Inc., New York, 1994.

10. Tagliaferre, Lewis, & Harbaugh, Gary L., Ph.D., **Recovery from Loss, A Personalized Guide to the Grieving Process**, Health Communications, Inc., Deerfield Beach, Florida, 1990.

11. Weiss, Brian L., M.D., **Many Lives, Many Masters**, A Fireside Book, Simon & Schuster, Inc. New York, 1988.

# About the Author

D AYLE E. SPENCER is best known for having been the founding Director of the Conflict Resolution Programs at the Carter Center of Emory University. She worked with former President Jimmy Carter for almost ten years to develop his approaches to negotiating and mediating international conflicts, including civil wars. Carter was awarded the Nobel Peace Prize for these efforts.

Ms. Spencer is a lawyer/negotiator who has organized negotiations between numerous governments and revolutionary leaders in civil war situations, including Ethiopia and Eritrea, Sudan and the Sudanese People's Liberation Front, and Liberia and the National Patriotic Front of Liberia. She is one of the few Americans to have negotiated with the government of North Korea and was instrumental in arranging for peace initiative undertaken by President Carter in that region. Her work in conflict resolution has taken her to over fifty countries on five continents where she has had hands-on involvement in a myriad of issues.

Prior to her pioneering work at the Carter Center, she served as an Assistant United States Attorney for the Northern, District of Alabama and was also law clerk to Chief Judge John R. Brown, of the Fifth US Circuit Court of Appeals in Houston, Texas.

For the past twenty years she has been Managing Director of the Pangaea Group, Inc., where she has served as a consultant to many Fortune 500 companies. Additionally, she and her husband, Will, co-direct the Maui Transitions Center where they assist adults in learning how to manage life's changes.

Dayle has been a frequent commentator on national news broadcasts, published in academic journals as well as authored a nationally syndicated news series on human rights in South Africa, and has tried approximately 100 jury trials in federal district court.

# Coming in 2015

## Loving Spirit,
## Self-help for the Journey of loss

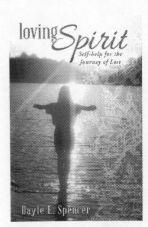

**A**S THE PERFECT companion to *Loving Allie, Transforming the Journey of Loss,* this inspirational workbook gives the reader the skills and insights to move beyond the throes of grief in a process that was developed over twenty years of working with clients in major life transitions.

This practical and compassionate guide empowers the reader to chart an individualized course to life beyond loss.

Share this book with anyone you love who has suffered a great loss in life.

To learn more about Dayle E. Spencer and her other products and services, including free resources and her blog, please visit her online.

**www.daylespencer.com**